Get the eBook FREE!

(PDF, ePub, Kindle, and liveBook all included)

We believe that once you buy a book from us, you should be able to read it in any format we have available. To get electronic versions of this book at no additional cost to you, purchase and then register this book at the Manning website.

Go to https://www.manning.com/freebook and follow the instructions to complete your pBook registration.

That's it!
Thanks from Manning!

T0073320

Full quotes from reviewers of *Demand Forecasting Best Practices*:

This new book continues to push the FVA mindset, illustrating practices that drive the efficiency and effectiveness of the business forecasting process.

—Michael Gilliland, Editor-in-Chief,
Foresight: Journal of Applied Forecasting

A must-read for any SCM professional, data scientist, or business owner. It's practical, accessible, and packed with valuable insights.

—Edouard Thieuleux, Founder of AbcSupplyChain

An exceptional resource that covers everything from basic forecasting principles to advanced forecasting techniques using artificial intelligence and machine learning. The writing style is engaging, making complex concepts accessible to both beginners and experts.

—Daniel Stanton, Mr. Supply Chain®

Nicolas did it again! Demand Forecasting Best Practices provides practical and actionable advice for improving the demand planning process.

—Spyros Makridakis, The Makridakis Open Forecasting Center,
Institute For the Future (IFF), University of Nicosia

This book is now my companion on all of our planning and forecasting projects. A perfect foundation for implementation and also to recommend process improvements.

—Werner Nindl, Chief Architect – CPM Practice Director, Pivotal Drive

This author understands the nuances of forecasting, and is able to explain them well.

—Burhan Ul Haq, Director of Products, Enablers

Both broader and deeper than I expected.

—Maxim Volgin, Quantitative Marketing Manager, KLM

Great book with actionable insights.

—Simon Tschöke, Head of Research, German Edge Cloud

Demand Forecasting Best Practices

NICOLAS VANDEPUT

MANNING
SHELTER ISLAND

brief contents

contents

preface

As COVID hit us in early 2020, I started training more companies on demand planning. Everyone realized at once that predicting future demand was critical for businesses. But challenging.

I have always been obsessed with continuous improvement and excellence. So, after each training course delivery or project, I took the opportunity to refine my approach to demand forecasting. Coaching teams across four continents and various industries made me realize that *demand planning excellence* can be boiled down to a set of best practices. Over time, I improved the methodology itself and how to explain it in a structured, straightforward way.

Pretty soon, I realized that I was starting all my projects with the same questions: Are you tracking forecast value added? How do you capture demand? Do you measure yourself against a benchmark? What is driving your demand? And I followed the same steps: collecting demand, determining the right forecasting granularity and horizon, testing out different models, implementing forecast value added, and so on.

Over time, I organized these questions and steps in a structured way: the *five-step framework to demand planning excellence*.

This book will guide you through these steps. Presenting you with the best practices to lead your demand planning process to excellence.

Feel free to share how you applied these ideas and techniques. You can reach me at nicolas.vandeput@supchains.com or on LinkedIn.

acknowledgments

For my third book, I could count on the amazing LinkedIn community to support me by reviewing my drafts. My warmest thanks go to the following people for their time and dedicated reviews.

Part 1 and Introduction, Slava Grinkevych, Jeff Carruthers, Jeffrey Connors, Adam Sobolewski, Damon DeWaide, Ryker Frandsen, Cassidy Williams, Zlata Jakubovic, William van den Bremer, Joel Martycz, Renaud Lecoeuche, Hugues d'Allest, Inigo Diaz, Marc Jacobs, Asmir Tandirević, Nicole Minskoff, Fabian Kleinschmidt, Chris Mousley, Agustin Peña Camprubi, Obinna Ikpengwa, and Mariano Ayerza.

Part 2, Leo Ducrot, Adam Sobolewski, Jeff Carruthers, Michael Ryan, Koen Cobbaert, Daniel Singer, Thamin Rashid, Lokesh Kamani, Pierre-Olivier Mazoyer, Rafael Vicco, Igor Henrique de Freitas, Emad Atef, Hammad Rafique, Daniel More, Tobias Faiß, Fabio Antonio Mangione, Tatiana Usuga, Mark Lado, Hernán David Pérez, Khem Singh Negi, Vi Dương, Mark Fox, Mohit Goyal, and Filip Nilsson.

Part 3 Michael Gilliland, Adam Sobolewski, Jeff Carruthers, Daniel Singer, Thamin Rashid, Pierre-Olivier Mazoyer, Lokesh Kamani, Mauricio Rendon Franco, and Léo Ducrot.

Part 4 and Conclusion, Koen Cobbaert, Slava Grinkevych, Hugues d'Allest, Cassidy Williams, Ryker Frandsen, Inigo Diaz, Fabian Kleinschmidt, Damon DeWaide, Michael Gilliland, and Agustin Pena.

I would also like to thank all Manning's reviewers for their insightful feedback and advise: Asif Iqbal, Brian Cocolicchio, Burhan Ul Haq, Gustavo Patino, Igor Dudchenko, Ike Okonkwo, Joaquin Beltran, Madhavan Ramani, Maxim Volgin, Oscar Cassetti, Philip Best, Richard Vaughan, Sanket Sharma, Simon Tschöke, Simone Sguazza, Srinivasan M, Sriram Macharla, and Werner Nindl.

I would especially like to thank Koen Cobbaert, Leo Ducrot, and Michael Gilliland for their long-time support—as always. Their insights proved invaluable.

Moreover, I would like to thank Manning's people for supporting me and the work we achieved together. Especially Ian Hough for the insightful reviews and as well as Andy Waldron for the opportunity and the support.

Finally, I would like to thank my friends and family for encouraging me with my endless projects.

about this book

This book was written for anyone who wants to improve their demand planning process. In particular, this book will help the following roles: demand planners, S&OP managers, supply chain leaders, and data scientists working on supply chain projects.

As a *demand planner,* you have many insights about your industry, products, and clients. You know your business. But you might face an inefficient demand planning process. Repetitive tasks—like manually filling up Excel files every month—slow you down and keep you away from more value-adding tasks. Discussions, negotiations, and political alignments between teams (such as sales and finance) might erode your overall forecasting accuracy as it diverts you from focusing on what drives business value.

By reading this book, you will learn:

- How to leverage tools and analytics to focus your work where you will have the most impact.
- How to use a forecasting model to create an accurate forecast baseline.
- How to manage stakeholders (sales, marketing, production, finance) and leverage their inputs.

As an *S&OP manager or supply chain leader,* you manage a team of professionals working on the demand planning process. You want to be sure that your demand forecast helps the other departments (sales, purchasing, manufacturing, logistics) make the right decisions. You need tools to assess whether the overall forecasting process is efficient and effective. You want your teams to focus on the most critical products (we will segment these in chapter 13). Moreover, you need insightful metrics to track your process quality (and forecast accuracy). In the end, you need to ensure that your forecasting process is done in the most efficient way and adds value to the supply chain.

You will learn:

- The appropriate forecasting granularity and horizon to use when forecasting demand.
- How to select appropriate forecasting metrics to track the quality of your demand planning process.
- How to use benchmarks to assess the efficacy and efficiency of your demand-planning process.
- How to segment your products to focus the work of your team where they will add the most value.
- When multiple teams review a forecast, how to promote ownership and accountability using the Forecast Value Added framework.

As a *data scientist* working on forecasting models, you need a dataset, a clear business objective (metrics, granularity, horizon), and a set of metrics to optimize. Unfortunately, data scientists often kickstart projects by jumping into creating models rather than spending time understanding the business requirements. This is what this book is about.

You will learn,

- To identify the business requirements when forecasting demand.
- Which data to feed to your model.
- Which metric(s) to use when assessing the quality of your model.
- Which demand drivers you could use in your model.

Note that this book will review the pros and cons of the different models you can use to forecast demand. But it will not cover how to make forecasting models. If you want to create your own models, I advise reading my previous book, *Data Science for Supply Chain Forecasting*.[1]

---

[1] (Vandeput, 2021)

How this book is organized: a roadmap

Let's take the time to outline our journey and the various questions we will discuss in this book.

Part 1 introduces us to forecasting demand:

- Chapter 1 has us begin our journey by introducing the demand planning excellence framework.
- Chapter 2 will address the important question of why we forecast demand and how it supports the overall supply chain.
- Chapters 3 and 4 will answer why and how we should forecast unconstrained demand rather than constrained sales.
- Chapters 5 and 6 will explore forecasting granularity and horizon.
- This part will conclude with a discussion on forecast reconciliations in chapter 7.

Part 2 focuses on how we can measure forecasting quality:

- Chapter 8 and 9 will start by introducing different forecasting KPIs (Bias, MAE, MAPE, RMSE) and discussing their pros and cons.
- Chapter 10 will answer a central question to demand planning: "What is a good level of forecast accuracy?" by using benchmarks.
- Chapter 11 will finish off this part by extending our KPIs to assess the forecasting quality of a whole product portfolio using value-weighted metrics.

Part 3 will cover the data-driven forecasting process:

- Chapter 12 will discuss the forecast value added framework that will allow you to track the added value of your whole forecasting process (leveraging the benchmarks and value-weighted metrics we discussed in part 2).
- Chapter 13 will explain how we can focus the work of demand parameters using segmentation techniques (such as ABC XYZ).

Part 4 will bring us to the end of the book, focusing on forecasting methods:

- Chapter 14 will cover statistical methods for demand forecasting.
- Chapter 15 will then cover advanced machine-learning techniques, comparing both ML and statistical approaches regarding complexity and expected results.
- Finally, we will discuss judgmental forecasts in chapter 16: when to use them and how to avoid intentional and unintentional biases.

liveBook discussion forum

Purchase of *Demand Forecasting Best Practices* includes free access to liveBook, Manning's online reading platform. Using liveBook's exclusive discussion features, you can attach comments to the book globally or to specific sections or paragraphs. It's a snap to make notes for yourself, ask and answer technical questions, and receive help from the author and other users. To access the forum, go to https://livebook.manning.com/book/demand-forecasting-best-practices/discussion. You can also learn more about Manning's forums and the rules of conduct at https://livebook.manning.com/discussion.

Manning's commitment to our readers is to provide a venue where a meaningful dialogue between individual readers and between readers and the author can take place. It is not a commitment to any specific amount of participation on the part of the author, whose contribution to the forum remains voluntary (and unpaid). We suggest you try asking the author some challenging questions lest his interest stray! The forum and the archives of previous discussions will be accessible from the publisher's website as long as the book is in print.

about the author

Nicolas Vandeput is a supply chain data scientist specializing in demand forecasting and inventory optimization. He founded his consultancy company, SupChains, in 2016; and an online platform for supply chain forecasting, SKU Science, in 2018. He always enjoys discussing new models and how to apply them to business reality. Passionate about education, Nicolas is both an avid learner and enjoys teaching at universities. Since 2020, he has been teaching demand forecasting and inventory optimization to master students in CentraleSupelec, Paris, France. He published *Data Science for Supply Chain Forecasting* in 2018 and *Inventory Optimization: Models and Simulations* in 2020.

about the cover illustration

The illustration on the cover of *Demand Forecasting Best Practices*, "Pythagoras of Crotona," by J. Augustus Knapp, is from *The Secret Teachings of all Ages* by Manly P. Hall, published in 1928. Hall's book is an encyclopedia of ancient occult and esoteric traditions of the world and explores topics ranging from alchemy to tarot, Egyptian mythology to Pythagorean philosophy.

Manning celebrates the inventiveness and initiative of the computer business with book covers based on the rich diversity of regional culture centuries ago, brought back to life by pictures from books such as this one.

Part 1

Forecasting demand

We start our journey by introducing the demand planning excellence framework (chapter 1). Then, we will discuss the most important elements of demand forecasting: why we forecast demand (chapter 2), why and how we should forecast unconstrained demand rather than constrained sales (chapters 3 and 4), and which granularity (chapter 5) and horizon (chapter 6) we should use and focus on when forecasting demand. Finally, we will discuss forecast reconciliations (chapter 7).

Demand forecasting excellence

Impossible to see, the future is.
—Yoda, Star Wars

1.1 Why do we forecast demand?

Supply chains are similar to living organisms making a multitude of daily decisions. It is an endless stream: how much, what, and where to buy, source, deliver, and store. To make appropriate decisions and weigh the pros and cons of potential outcomes, we need both qualitative and quantitative insights. In supply chains, these decisions ultimately depend on expected revenues and underlying costs (fixed and variable). At the core of these decisions lies the question of how much demand you can expect in the future. The better you can estimate it, the better your decisions.

In short, supply chains are about making decisions. And demand planners are there to provide meaningful, actionable information to support these. Better forecasting will allow your supply chain to face streamlined operations, fewer shortages, less useless inventory, and more sales. Ultimately, fewer costs and more profits. In some cases—for example, when supply is constrained—better forecasting will result in a competitive advantage as you can better prepare for the future. We can picture a demand planner as a sailor on a boat with a spyglass. You want to bring relevant information about what's on the horizon to your comrades on the ship—leaving them to decide what's best to do.

This book will take you on a journey towards demand planning excellence (figure 1.1). The objective is not to work harder but to work smarter. We will aim for efficiency, efficacy, and focus. As you progress through the book, you will be able to implement new best practices in your demand planning process while challenging the status quo. Data, metrics, process, models, people: no stone will be left unturned. These best practices will allow you to improve the quality of your forecasts to deliver more value to your supply chain and support your colleagues to make better, more informed decisions.

Figure 1.1   Demand planning excellence: efficacy and efficiency

Throughout the book, I will explain these best practices step by step, highlighting how they will lead you to efficacy (more useful forecasts) and efficiency (reducing your team's workload while making the most out of their available time). Each chapter will be another opportunity for you to improve your forecasting process and make your forecasts more useful for your supply chain.

The best practices, tips, and tricks I share in this book are anchored in my experience advising supply chains around the globe.[1] Even if these best practices are widely applicable, the particular implementation will change from company to company—mostly depending on your business drivers, your team's maturity, and the data you have access to. Moreover, I will highlight many widespread bad practices throughout the book, explaining how they are inconsistent with process excellence. Practitioners should quit them.

---

[1]   Most data, figures, and cases shown in this book are directly inspired by real client cases (all numbers have been changed).

1.2 *Five steps to demand planning excellence*

Demand forecasts are used to support supply chain decisions (how much to order, produce, or move). I define demand planning excellence as a combination of efficacy (your forecasts help decision-making) and efficiency (you spend as little time as possible working on these forecasts).[2]

In this book, I will show you how to set up your demand planning process using an original 5-step framework (figure 1.2). Forecasts should:

- Be done at the right aggregation level and on the right time horizon.
- Leverage appropriate data.
- Monitored using relevant metrics.
- Rely on appropriate models to generate a forecast baseline.
- Be enriched by an efficient review process.

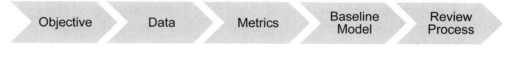

Figure 1.2   5-step framework for demand planning excellence

As you use this framework, and all its underlying concepts and best practices, you will be able to set up a tailor-made process aiming for demand planning excellence. I like to use this framework to kick off and organize my forecasting projects. So should you.

Before jumping into these best practices, let's take the time to outline our journey throughout the five steps and the various questions we will discuss in this book. Note that the chapters follow a path to simplify your learning journey—They do not always strictly stick to the chronology of the demand planning excellence framework.

1.2.1 *Objective. What do you need to forecast?*

A forecast is a piece of information that various teams in the supply chain will use to make smart decisions (chapter 2). When discussing demand planning improvement with clients, I always start with why. "*Why do you forecast demand? What decisions are you supporting with this forecast?*" This should be your starting point too. (Answering these two main questions will also answer a third

---

[2] Note that I didn't include accuracy in this statement on purpose. Forecasting accuracy is a non-sufficient condition for a forecast to be useful. You could have a forecast that is both accurate but useless. This could be, for example, because it is not done on the right granularity or does not use the appropriate demand data. A forecast needs multiple conditions to be useful—accuracy is only one of them. Accuracy shouldn't be your main goal. Usefulness should be.

one: "*Who will use this forecast?*") Knowing the types of decisions your supply chain needs to make (e.g., how much to produce, where to deploy inventory, whether to open or close plants) is the first step of the 5-step framework. Based on these decisions, we will assess the relevant material and temporal aggregation levels (chapter 5) as well as the forecasting horizon (chapter 6). We will also discuss how different teams might have to use different forecasting models and processes (chapter 7).

1.2.2   *Data. What data do you need to support your forecasting model and process?*

The most critical data to collect is unconstrained demand rather than constrained sales (chapters 2 and 3). Moreover, you will also need to assess what external drivers impact your demand (such as promotions, pricing, or product launches) and start collecting this data as well (chapter 14).

1.2.3   *Metrics. How do you evaluate forecasting quality?*

First, you will need to select relevant metrics to assess your forecasting quality. We will discuss accuracy and bias in chapters 8 and 9. In chapter 10, you will learn how to assess if your forecasting model and process are achieving satisfactory accuracy thanks to benchmarks. In chapter 11, we will refine our metrics to cope with broad product portfolios.

1.2.4   *Baseline model. How do you create an accurate, automated forecast baseline?*

You do not want your demand planning team to generate (and review) every single forecast by hand. Instead, to reduce human work to the minimum, you want to use a forecasting model as powerful as possible to generate a forecast baseline. This model should leverage a wide range of insights (such as promotions and other demand drivers). To create this baseline, you can use time series models (chapter 14), predictive models (chapter 14), or machine learning (chapter 15).

1.2.5   *Review Process. How to review the baseline forecast, and who should do it?*

Once the baseline forecast is generated by your forecasting engine, the enrichment phase can begin: various teams will review the forecast and suggest modifications. These suggestions should improve the baseline forecast because they bring human expertise and insights to which the model doesn't have access (chapter 16). The cornerstone of this review process should be the forecast value added (FVA) framework. It promotes ownership and accountability (chapter 12) by tracking each team's modifications to the baseline forecast and measuring how much they improved (or worsened) it. Using this framework, you will achieve unprecedented levels of efficiency and efficacy. On the other side, if you overlook it, be ready to face influence wars (chapter 16) and inefficiencies. Finally, chapter 13 will discuss how to reduce your teams' workload by focusing their work on the most critical products and those for which they are most likely to add value.

Let's recap with three examples:

- *Short-term forecast:* Let's imagine you need to decide what to ship to your stores every week. The forecast could be updated every week, with a horizon of a few weeks forward. The granularity would be SKU per store.[3] Because you need to populate the forecast every week, the time to review it will be limited. Henceforth, only a few demand planners should validate it and focus on only the products where they are the most likely to add value (chapter 13). As explained in chapter 15, machine learning models should typically be preferred here because they can leverage different granular insights (promotions, prices, shortages, weather) and allow demand-planning staff to prioritize other forecasts that require more qualitative insights.

- *Mid-term forecast:* You want to assess what to produce in the coming months. This is your typical S&OP forecast where you need to gather inputs from many stakeholders (sales, finance, marketing, planners, clients, suppliers). The forecast can be generated (and its accuracy measured) at a global level per SKU and once per month using value-weighted metrics (chapter 11). You will have to track forecast value added (chapter 12) to ensure everyone contributes to better forecasts while avoiding inherent functional bias (chapter 16).

- *Long-term forecast:* You need to set the budget for the upcoming year. This is a long-term, aggregated forecast (most likely done at a value/revenue level per brand/segmented). To create various scenarios (based on pricing, marketing, or new product introduction), you will want to use a causal model where the weight of inputs can be set and discussed (chapter 14). You will also have to follow best practices to leverage your team's insights and avoid intentional and cognitive biases (chapter 16).

---

[3] SKU stands for *Stock Keeping Unit.* It denotes a distinct type of item (usually a combination of product, packaging, and bulk size) in which inventory and production are managed.

Summary

- There are five steps to demand planning excellence: identify your objective; decide what data you need; understand how to evaluate the quality of your forecasting; create an accurate baseline model; and understand how to review the baseline forecast.
- *Objective:* Always start by asking, why do you need to forecast demand, and what decisions are you supporting with this forecast?
- *Data:* Collect data on unconstrained demand, as well as data on external drivers that impact your demand.
- *Metrics:* Accuracy and bias must be considered.
- *Baseline Model:* Use a forecasting model as powerful as possible to generate a forecast baseline and reduce the need for manual human efforts
- *Review process:* Understand where to prioritize efforts, and what sort of forecast will provide the most value: short-term, mid-term, or long-term forecasting?

Introduction to demand forecasting

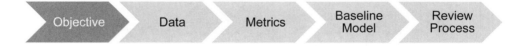

As highlighted in the 5-step framework above, this chapter will begin our improvement journey by discussing the objective of demand planning. Before jumping into how to make a good forecast, we need to understand why we forecast demand in the first place.

2.1 Why do we forecast demand?

Making smart decisions requires insights. Imagine you want to buy a house. You will want to know the current state of the house, if you should plan for significant expenses, the neighborhood's current prices, how they will evolve in the future, and so on. In supply chains, most decisions—how much to buy, produce, ship, and store—rely (at least partially) on demand forecasts. As you have a better idea of your clients' future behaviors and needs, you can make better decisions. This will ultimately result in higher service level, better production and supply plans, less waste, and lower overall costs.

To summarize, as demand planners, our objective is to make the best possible demand forecasts so other teams can make better decisions.

Forecasting demand is always a means to an end, not the end itself.
The end is to help decision-makers by providing them with helpful information.

2.2   Definitions

Before diving further into demand forecasting, we must define a few confusing terms: demand, sales, demand forecast, sales targets, financial budget, and supply planning. Many supply chains are, unfortunately, forecasting sales rather than demand. And, as you will see in this chapter, sales forecasting is a bad practice, often resulting in politics, wishful thinking, and a vicious supply-sales circle.

2.2.1   Demand, sales, and supply

Demand is formally defined as *what* your customers want, *when* they want it, and *how much* they want. This is an *unconstrained* point of view: your customers might want to have some products right now, even if you don't have these products in stock.

Imagine the following situation: you are responsible for an ice cream truck selling ice creams to kids (figure 2.1).

Figure 2.1   You sell ice creams

In this case, demand would be the type of ice cream that the kids dream about while queuing. The demand forecast is how much you think future demand will be. It is a prediction. For example, "I think that kids will want to eat 15 chocolate ice creams tomorrow" is a demand forecast. Sales happen when demand and supply match: your clients want something, and you have pieces in stock (figure 2.2).

Figure 2.2 Demand, supply, and sales

WHY YOU SHOULD NEVER FORECAST SALES

On the other hand, sales are *constrained* by (lack of) supply[4]. Forecasting *constrained* sales instead of *unconstrained* demand will result in a vicious circle where any shortage is likely to lead to a perpetual out-of-stock situation, as illustrated in figure 2.3.

Figure 2.3 Sales forecasting resulting in a vicious circle

---

[4] I use here the terms "constrained sales" and "unconstrained demand" to emphasize the difference between the two. Conceptually, I make no difference between "constrained sales" and "sales" nor between "unconstrained demand" and "demand".

Let's illustrate this vicious circle using the ice cream example. Imagine that you are currently out of stock of chocolate ice cream:

- What will be the *sales* of chocolate ice cream tomorrow?
  None, as you have no inventory.
- What will be the *demand* for chocolate ice cream tomorrow?
  Probably *some*, as usual.

Now, imagine that your purchasing manager uses your constrained sales forecast to reorder ice cream. Because you didn't forecast any sales for the chocolate flavor, the purchasing manager won't replenish any from the supplier. Because you won't receive any supply of chocolate ice cream, you won't sell any in the future. And you will continue to forecast zero sales. You are experiencing the sales forecasting vicious circle.

As you follow this sales forecasting approach, your forecasting accuracy will be 100% (you forecast 0, you sell 0—that's perfectly accurate). Similarly, suppose the inventory manager tracks adherence to stock targets. They will also achieve 100% adherence: the forecast is 0, so they want to have 0 pieces in stock. And they have zero pieces in stock. Inventory is on target! You will both achieve a 100% success rate in your respective KPIs, but it won't result in any good business outcomes.

On the other hand, by forecasting *unconstrained* demand, you will replenish the right products and satisfy your clients.

To properly forecast demand (rather than sales), we need to answer two questions:

- How do we track demand rather than sales? We will discuss this in chapter 3.
- If you cannot track demand due to shortages, how should you forecast demand when facing historical shortages? We will discuss this in chapters 3 and 14.

CONSTRAINING YOUR DEMAND FORECAST INTO A SALES FORECAST

As discussed, unconstrained demand forecasts should be the information communicated to the other teams to make their decisions. But businesses will also get insights from looking at their expected sales and revenue figures. To transform your demand forecast into a sales (or revenue) forecast, you need to constrain it based on expected shortages and weight it based on the expected sales prices as highlighted in figure 2.4.

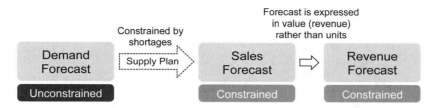

Figure 2.4 Demand forecast and expected revenues

For example, you forecasted an unconstrained demand for 10 pieces of chocolate ice cream for the upcoming week. You will communicate this information to your purchasing colleagues (so they can replenish you with the right amount). Then, looking at your current inventory (zero), you understand that you face a shortage and therefore forecast zero sales and revenues for the week to come. This sales forecast might then be communicated to your finance team.

2.2.2   *Supply plan, financial budget, and sales targets*

Professionals usually confuse demand forecasts with supply plans, financial budgets, and sales targets. Let's highlight the differences one by one.

SUPPLY PLAN

A supply chain's (supply) plan indicates how much it is planning on producing, buying, and shipping. Basically, this plan will drive the whole production and logistic flow. The supply plan results from the demand forecast and other inputs, such as logistic constraints and inventory stock targets. But this supply plan is *not* the demand forecast: you can forecast X and produce Y. For example, you could expect a demand of 10 pieces of ice cream, decide to supply 15 pieces (to be on the safe side), and ultimately only sell eight pieces (forecast = 10, supply plan = 15, sales = 8). Remember, we create a demand forecast to help our colleagues from supply to make the best possible supply plan (figure 2.5).

Figure 2.5   Demand forecast, supply plans, and sales

A demand planner is like a sailor on a boat looking at the horizon with a spyglass. Looking at the horizon in a spyglass is not the same as being active on the deck taking action. The sailor looking at the horizon should provide the most accurate information to the rest of the crew while not biasing it. Based on this information, it is then up to the sailors on the deck to take action.

FINANCIAL BUDGET

A company's financial budget is usually created once a year during an often-grueling process (that sometimes gets political). This budget contains expected expenses and revenues. Expected revenues are directly connected to expected sales, and expected sales are directly related to expected demand. But sales forecasting (and cash-flow projections) is not the same as demand forecasting. Sales forecasts are constrained by supply and inventory. In contrast, demand forecasts are unconstrained and represent your clients' expected demand (regardless of whether you have inventory or not).

If you want to use your unconstrained demand forecast as a baseline for your financial budget, you will need to constrain it based on expected shortages and weight it based on the expected sales prices, as explained in the previous section.

Unfortunately, many planners will use the financial budget as a baseline for their demand forecasts. This will result in wishful thinking and might be a significant source of judgmental bias, undermining your overall forecasting accuracy (see more about this in chapter 16).

SALES TARGETS

Many businesses communicate sales targets to their sales teams to incentivize them to sell more: reaching their targets will grant them a bonus. Sales targets are basically a sales and marketing policy, executed along with HR, to reward and motivate sales teams.

For example, you could forecast a demand of 10 pieces of ice cream; decide to supply 15 pieces; and give a bonus to your sales team if they sell more than 12 pieces (forecast = 10, plan = 15, sales target = 12).

These sales targets often result in political conflicts over demand forecasts as salespeople will want forecasts to be as low as possible to make sales targets easier to beat (more about this later in chapter 16). To continue with the previous example, a salesperson might try to convince you to reduce the demand forecast to 7 pieces while maintaining the supply plan as high as possible. By doing so, the sales target will also be decreased to 9 pieces. Salespeople might want management expectations to be as low as possible while enjoying plenty of supply so they can sell as much as possible. At a higher level, sales targets (or budget) can be set to show a path to growth goals that have been shared with key shareholders or investors.

Summary

- Demand forecasting is about getting an unconstrained picture of your clients' wishes (what they want, how much they want, when they want it).

- A demand forecast is a piece of information that will serve as input for the supply plan, financial budget, and sales targets.

- A demand forecast isn't a plan, an objective, or a cash-flow income prediction.

Capturing unconstrained demand (and not sales)

As we discussed in chapter 2, supply chains need to forecast demand and not sales (*Objective*). Unfortunately, capturing actual unconstrained demand can be incredibly challenging, if not impossible. This chapter focuses on the second step of the demand planning excellence framework: how to collect accurate demand data.

Remember, unconstrained demand is defined as your clients' initially requested product, quantity, and delivery date (what, how much, when). Demand is *not* measured as the number of actual sales which are constrained by inventory at hand (or, more generally, by supply availability). In other words, demand is about what your clients want, how much they want, and when they want it. Not what you shipped, how much you shipped, and when you shipped it (or invoiced).

Most companies do not record demand but sales. As long as you have enough inventory on hand, all incoming demand will result in sales. So, tracking sales—and not demand directly—is ok, *as long as* you do not face any shortage. In our earlier ice cream example, if the kids want chocolate ice cream (demand), and you have some in your freezer (supply), you can sell them (sales).

You will start facing demand collection issues when you're out of stock.

In this chapter and the following, I will present you with four techniques to collect unconstrained demand in case of shortages:

- Order collection and management (section 3.1)
- Shortage-censoring (section 3.2)
- Aggregate forecasting to cope with substitution and cannibalization (section 3.3)
- Customer collaboration (chapter 4)

By using these techniques, you will be able to improve your demand data quality. Perfect demand collection is very likely to be impossible. But each step towards better data will result in a better forecast. Simply put:

- More data = better forecast (we will discuss demand drivers in chapter 14)
- Better data = better forecast

Moreover, unconstraining demand will allow you to estimate your lost sales and the impact of shortages on top-line revenue.

Experience

As a consultant, I developed a forecasting model for a manufacturing company. I optimized it down to the last 0.1% accuracy, squeezing every drop of accuracy. As I was discussing demand data quality with my client, they told me that I received a dataset from their new IT system. And that they reported results using another dataset from an older system. I suspected a discrepancy between both datasets. So, we tried to compare and reconcile them. To our surprise, we saw an initial discrepancy of around 5% spread over all the products! We could reduce the difference down to 1% but couldn't explain the remaining discrepancies. I stopped working on improving the forecasting model to get another 0.1% accuracy.

3.1 Order collection and management

In case of shortages, you can use an order management system to deal with incoming orders and client requests. By doing so, you will continue to collect demand even if your outbound shipments drop.

You will need to track different types of orders:

- *Open orders:* These are the orders that aren't delivered yet—most likely because you do not have the required goods on hand currently. You need to keep a backlog of these open orders and update your clients about them. Your message should be along these lines, "We recorded your order. We'll ship it when we have inventory. We should have inventory within two weeks." If you do not track properly open orders (or do not communicate about them), you risk *order duplication.*

- *Duplicated orders:* If you do not keep a backlog of open orders, your clients might reorder the same order multiple times until it is fulfilled. As you record each incoming order as a new one, you will capture over-inflated demand.

- *Canceled orders:* Some clients will cancel their orders because you can't serve them in time. You need to track these orders (especially their initially requested delivery dates) and their *reason for cancellation*[5].

- *Substitution orders:* Some customers will decide to buy another product instead of their initial choice if it is unavailable. You will need to track these substitution orders separately because demand should be allocated to the initial product rather than to the sold product. If an order can't be fulfilled, your order management system should automatically propose a substitute (or another shipping location). You should avoid any manual input, which will often result in (precious) information getting lost.

We also need to consider *uncollected orders.* Some clients intended to make an order but did not commit because inventory was missing. Uncollected (or abandoned) orders can be seen as an extreme version of canceled orders. Think about all the online carts that will never get to check-out because the products are out-of-stock. Nevertheless, these uncollected orders must also be incorporated into your total unconstrained demand. Unfortunately, uncollected demand is especially difficult to track and estimate (as, by definition, it is not recorded).

Moreover, if stock availability is a critical sales factor in your industry (which is often the case for retailers), you might be dealing with a lot of uncollected orders. We will discuss how to deal with uncollected orders in section 3.2, where we will discuss *shortage-censoring.* Remember, you need to record each order's

---

[5] I usually advise supply chains to use a few categories to track reasons for cancellation (such as "pricing is too high", "delay is too long", "client doesn't need it anymore", "used substitution product". Avoid "Client Cancelation" because that is too vague). Using too many categories will confuse customer service teams. On the other hand, you need to use enough categories to get meaningful business insights.

initial requested delivery date. Not the date the order was input, not the shipping date, not the invoicing date. Moreover, ensure that your client service teams do not change orders' data (especially dates) to show artificially high service levels. I like to call this behavior data or KPI hacking. This will only result in lower data quality, resulting in less relevant forecasts and, ultimately, poorer decisions.

3.2 Shortage-Censoring and Uncollected Orders

Most B2C businesses (and many B2B businesses) won't be able to collect their clients' orders in case of shortages.

On the other hand, sales and demand are equivalent when there is no shortage. Tracking *when* you are out of stock will allow you to know when demand and sales are not aligned. Figure 3.1 shows an example where you can see the impact of product availability on sales. By tracking both inventory and sales over time, we can highlight periods where we know the actual unconstrained demand (when stock is available). And periods where we only see constrained sales (in this example, sales drop to zero when there is a shortage).

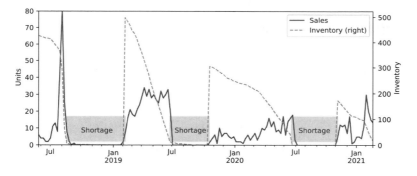

Figure 3.1   Sales vs. inventory for a product sold online

Your forecasting engine can then use this out-of-stock information to censor relevant periods (see more about this in chapter 14). The model should acknowledge that sales are constrained during out-of-stock periods and not be fooled by low sales numbers.

In some specific cases, you might have to censor periods even if you have inventory left. For example, if your inventory count isn't accurate enough, you might be experiencing shortages *even* if your ERP system display products on stock. In retail, you might have a few pieces left in stock, but none of them are displayed on shelves to customers. With ultra-fresh products, clients might prefer competition if the freshness of your products isn't satisfactory.

Leveraging information about historical shortage periods is usually your best bet to unconstrained sales. Unfortunately, in practice, information about inventory levels is nearly never used by modern forecast engines—even though the data is often readily available. It is time supply chains start using smarter engines.

3.2.1 *Using demand drivers to forecast historical demand*

If you want to better assess historical demand (and estimate lost sales), you can leverage demand drivers that aren't impacted by lack of inventory (such as weather, web traffic, or the number of people visiting a store) to *retrospectively* estimate demand during shortages. There's more about demand drivers in chapter 14.

Let's imagine that you are responsible for an ice cream truck. You would usually sell a waffle cone for every fifth client who places an order. If you ran out of waffle cones at 2 PM and subsequently, 25 clients took ice creams between 2 PM and 6 PM, you know that you could have sold around five more waffle cones on this day. You can then extrapolate unconstrained demand numbers using this projection on top of the morning's sales.

3.3   *Substitution and cannibalization*

Being out-of-stock on one product might result in higher sales for *another* product as your clients have to fall back on similar products (figure 3.2).

Figure 3.2   Choosing a product of substitution

This effect is called *substitution*: it will result in more sales than (original) demand for the substitute and fewer sales than demand for the substituted product. In our example from figure 3.2, you will have more sales than demand for vanilla ice cream but fewer sales than demand for chocolate ice cream.

On the other hand, *cannibalization* happens when you run a promotion on a product, resulting in lower sales and demand for similar items. Cannibalization could also occur when launching new products (figure 3.3).

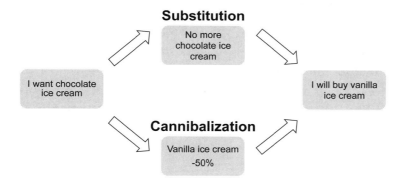

Figure 3.3   Substitution versus cannibalization

In both cases, if you forecast sales rather than demand, you will end up over forecasting the wrong product (that benefited from the substitution/cannibalization) and under-forecasting the second.

The impact of product substitution and cannibalization is especially complicated to consider when forecasting demand. One potential solution is to forecast demand at the family level rather than per product. For example, by forecasting demand of ice creams (in general) rather than forecasting demand for chocolate and vanilla ice creams separately. (This technique is called top-down forecasting, we will discuss it further in chapter 5.) Unfortunately, this technique is not a silver bullet against product substitution and cannibalization and will come with its challenges:

- We assume that products of the same family are suitable substitutes. Unfortunately, defining such families is not a trivial task. Looking back at our ice cream example, should you divide your ice creams into two sub-families: fruits and non-fruits perfumes? Or should you do it per positioning (premium vs. budget)? Or per packaging (scoop vs. cones)?
- You will have to pay careful attention when splitting family-forecasts into SKU-forecasts. Imagine the following scenario: one stock keeping unit (SKU) was recently out-of-stock. If you disaggregate a family forecast based on recent sales, this recent shortage will impact the split and allocate a lower forecast to this particular SKU. (More about top-down forecasts in chapter 5.) This will result in less stock deployed for this SKU, kickstarting the sales forecasting vicious circle we discussed in chapter 2.

Summary

- You need to forecast demand and not sales; forecasting sales is likely to lead to misleading predictions.
- Capturing clients' unconstrained demand can be challenging.
- If you can't set up a proper order management system (collecting orders in a backlog in case of shortage), you should censor historical shortages in your dataset when forecasting.
- Some forecasting techniques might help to unconstrain historical sales to assess the number of lost sales you suffered and better approximate historical demand.

Collaboration: data sharing and planning alignment

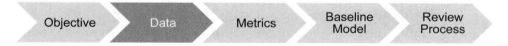

Objective | Data | Metrics | Baseline Model | Review Process

As discussed in the previous chapter, collecting demand data is key to proper demand forecasting but especially challenging. In this chapter, we will discuss how you can collaborate with your clients to improve your data quality and directly look into the demand they are facing from their customers.

4.1 How supply chains distort demand information

Let's imagine a simplistic supply chain with a manufacturer, a retailer, and end consumers, as illustrated in figure 4.1. This is called a two-echelons supply chain because we have two stages (the manufacturer and the retailer).

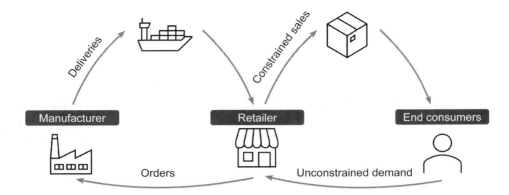

Figure 4.1   Simple supply chain with two echelons

In this example, the retailer faces unconstrained demand coming from end consumers. That's the flow of information that the global supply chain should forecast. Anything else is planning.

Unfortunately, in case of shortage, the retail store can only record the constrained sales—resulting in a loss of information. (As discussed in chapter 3, there are a few possibilities on how to unconstraint this data: order collection and management, shortage-censoring, and aggregated forecasting.)

If you put yourself in the manufacturer's shoes, the orders you receive from the retailer aren't perfectly correlated with the retailer's constrained sales (as illustrated in figure 4.2). These orders are even less correlated with the end consumers' demand. Indeed, it is the retailer's inventory policy that is driving the orders sent to the manufacturer. Namely, how the retailer wants to place its orders: full pallets? Full truck loads? Monthly orders? And how it manages its inventory targets. For example, suppose the retailer decides to change its policy from keeping two weeks stock, up to three weeks of stock. That will result in a massive order to the manufacturer without any connection to any change in the end demand.

On top of that, in case of shortage, many manufacturers will struggle to track incoming orders properly. In practice, most manufacturers base their forecasts directly on their deliveries.

Figure 4.2 Loss of information quality along the supply chain

To conclude, as shown in figure 4.2, each extra step in a supply chain is likely to distort the flow of information initiated by the end customers. A bit like the children's game telephone where each player has to repeat a message to the next one—until the final message is unrecognizable.

4.2   *Bullwhip effect*

As shown in figure 4.3, the bullwhip effect[6] describes a situation where the more upstream an echelon is in the supply chain, the more demand variation it faces, even if the final demand (from end customers) is steady. In our earlier example, the manufacturer might see lots of variations in the order pattern of the retailer even though the end consumer demand is stable. Overall, the more upstream a node is, the more pronounced the effect.

The name "bullwhip" comes from the fact that a small deviation of the final customer demand will produce a large variability at the manufacturer's end. Just like cracking a whip with a fast flick of the wrist.

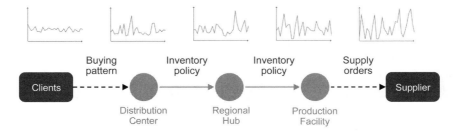

Figure 4.3   Bullwhip effect (the local sales pattern is illustrated above each stage; this is an illustration from my book *Inventory Optimization: Models and Simulations*).[7]

---

[6]   The bullwhip effect was initially theorized in the 1960s by Jay Forrester (professor at MIT). It got more attention in the late 1990s, when the name "bullwhip" was bestowed by Procter & Gamble (P&G) management team. P&G observed that, despite the fact that the final demand for Pampers was stable (babies consumed a steady flow), the orders at the manufacturing sites were highly variable.

[7]   Vandeput, 2020.

As identified by Lee et al. (1997), there are four main causes of the bullwhip effect:

- Order forecasting
- Order batching
- Price fluctuation and promotions
- Shortage gaming

To these initial four causes, I like to add another one: lead time variation. I will discuss it at the end of this section.

These five effects are not independent. On the contrary, they tend to reinforce each other in a vicious circle. Let's investigate them one by one.

4.2.1   Order forecasting

Order forecasting means forecasting incoming direct orders rather than the final client demand. (In the earlier example from figure 4.1, the manufacturer is forecasting incoming orders rather than actual demand.) We could call this double guessing: because you do not know the demand your client is facing, you have to guess it based on their ordering pattern. As each node in the global supply chain forecasts incoming orders, they will tend to distort the incoming demand signal and most likely overreact.[8]

ORDER FORECASTING AND INVENTORY POLICIES

Worse, inventory policies will have a multiplication effect on the demand forecast.

Let's illustrate this with an example (see figure 4.4): Let's imagine the following case, you face a steady 100 units per week demand coming from your end consumers. You keep a stock target of four weeks of inventory, and you order around 100 units per week from your manufacturer (100×4=400 units).

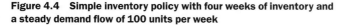

Figure 4.4   Simple inventory policy with four weeks of inventory and a steady demand flow of 100 units per week

---

[8]   The beer game—a supply chain simulation game—allows players to experience the bullwhip effect. In this game, each player manages one node of a 4-echelon beer supply. Players have to manage their orders and inventory levels while having no information about the final demand and only seeing the direct incoming orders. The game was initially developed by Jay Forrester (from MIT) in the 1960s. It was codified later in its "modern" setup in Sterman (1992). You can play a free online version of this game using this link: https://beergame.opexanalytics.com/#/

Let's now imagine that you think that the end consumer demand decreased by 10% per week (to 90 units), as shown in figure 4.5. Your current inventory target is around four weeks of inventory. Hence, you estimate to have 40 units too much in stock (you currently have 400 pieces in stock and want to have 360). So, as you stick to your inventory policy, you will decrease your next order by 50 units (40 units because of overstock and 10 units because of your reduced forecast).

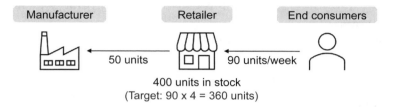

Figure 4.5   As demand decreases by 10%, the new order is mechanically reduced by 50%

In turn, your direct supplier will see a massive order reduction compared to your usual order pattern (from the regular 100 units to an expected order of 50 units). This might result in an even steeper order decrease from your manufacturer to its own suppliers. And so on. In short, the slightest final client demand variation results in a massive variation at the manufacturer's end.

Forecasting final clients' demand directly is particularly critical when the supply chain includes multiple echelons (and actors). Supply chains that can accurately react as they see the final client demand changing, and not overreact because one of their chain links changes its ordering policy, will get a definitive edge over siloed competitors. (We will discuss collaboration frameworks in section 4.3.) Remember, if you can forecast the end customer demand, everything else is planning.

4.2.2   Order batching

Usually, the more upstream a node is in the overall supply chain, the bigger its batch size (or the longer its order review period). Sales and purchasing conditions promoting bigger orders (such as discounts for full truckloads) will push this effect further. Overall, as we move upstream in the supply chain, we face fewer but bigger orders. This results in a lumpier order signal. Moreover, batch ordering will delay information as outbound orders are delayed compared to incoming demand. In short, order batching is delaying and distorting the demand information signal.

4.2.3   *Price fluctuation and promotions*

Promotions and price fluctuations distort demand. Unfortunately, the various upstream stakeholders in a supply chain are often not aware of price changes or promotions done by retailers and distributors. Instead, they will observe swinging incoming volumes (without knowing the specific underlying reasons). Promotions can also force manufacturing to produce goods months in advance to compensate for the lack of production flexibility and capacity. We will discuss how forecasting models can cope with promotions and price changes in chapter 14.

Walmart is a famous counter-example. By keeping promotions to a minimum and always striving to keep stable low prices, they enjoy a relatively stable demand and minimize the bullwhip effect passed on to their suppliers.

4.2.4   *Shortage gaming*

In some cases, when the supply chain is very siloed, each node might place oversized orders in a rogue move to protect itself against a speculative future supply shortage. This will often happen in times of supply crisis (e.g., Coronavirus). Shortage gaming will be done at the expense of other nodes that will suffer from supply shortages. At the same time, the one node that ordered too much will suffer from excess inventory. This cycle of speculative orders and shortages is often a self-fulfilling prophecy. Shortage gaming can also happen at the very end of a supply chain when final customers fear that they will lack supply. We observed this effect during the coronavirus with toilet paper runs (these runs are often self-fulfilling prophecies).

> **Experience**
>
> I witnessed this specific issue in a distribution company with one central warehouse and multiple (independent) stores. If an independent retailer suspected a potential shortage for one of its top sellers (or any trendy new product), it would try to capture as much inventory as possible from the central warehouse to protect itself. This behavior increased stress and resentment among employees and ultimately resulted in lower sales (as one shop had excess inventory while others suffered shortages).

4.2.5   *Lead time variations*

As suppliers' lead times vary, clients react.

As presented in my book *Inventory Optimization: Models and Simulations*, stock targets are related to the expected demand deviation (or forecast error) over the risk-horizon (lead times plus review periods). To put it simply, if your supplier quoted you a lead time of 21 days, your safety stocks should protect you over the expected demand variation during the 21 days. Let's imagine that your supplier announces a delay and informs you that it will now take 28 days to deliver your products. You will want more safety stocks—you need to be protected over a longer risk-horizon. You will order more.

Let's imagine a worse scenario. You are responsible for the supply chain of an American-based distributor of Chinese-produced goods. Chinese ports are overloaded: too much traffic, not enough capacity. Your supplier announces that going forward, all lead times should be increased by one month. How will you react? Longer (more variable) lead times mean that you want to have even more inventory to protect your supply chain. So, you will order more from your supplier to build up your safety stocks. Maybe, you want to be on the safe side in case even longer delays are announced and will order even more. At the same time, thousands of American-based planners are thinking the same, and doing the same. As a result, the pressure on Chinese manufacturers and logistics centers is ever-growing, resulting in longer lead times. It's an endless loop (figure 4.6).

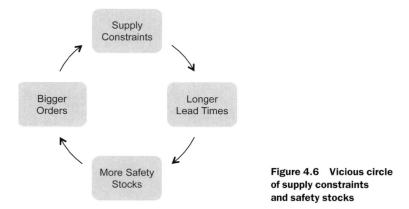

Figure 4.6 Vicious circle of supply constraints and safety stocks

The opposite effect will also take place. If your supplier announces shorter lead times, you will reduce your safety stocks and be left with overstocks. In turn, your supplier will also face lower orders as it reduces its lead times.

We have now looked at all of the contributing factors that feed into the bullwhip effect. This effect is not a fatality. It can be prevented because supply chains have tools at their disposal to dampen it—or get rid of it entirely—while aligning their planning with their clients and suppliers. We will discuss these techniques in detail in the next section.

4.3   Collaborative planning

In this section, we will discuss *collaborative* planning: instead of working in silos (by forecasting direct incoming orders and making supply orders without consideration for the other supply chain's echelons), we will share information and align our plans with our clients and suppliers.

Let's first discuss *internal* collaboration (collaboration within your supply chain) and then *external* collaboration (collaboration with your clients and suppliers).

4.3.1   Internal collaboration

Before looking at collaborating with your clients and suppliers, you can align your supply chain internally. Depending on your maturity and integration level, you might have to start by enabling *end-to-end visibility*. Then you can move on with *end-to-end planning and control*. Looking at both in more detail:

1   *End-to-end visibility:* As the most critical building block for enabling end-to-end internal collaboration, you need to establish a global view of demand (and supply) across each inventory node in your supply chain. Leveraging more insights and data (local shortages, sell-outs, point-of-sale data) will allow you to improve the quality of your forecasts. Moreover, you could use this data to create (advanced) reports, but reporting won't assure or enable alignment.

2   *End-to-end control and planning:*

   a   *Demand forecasting:* Orchestrate pricing, promotions, and marketing across nodes (i.e., channels, markets, . . .) based on supply and inventory availability. This will usually be done through the S&OP cycle.

   b   *Supply and inventory planning:* Have a central team responsible for setting inventory policies across your supply chain, and ensure that these policies are followed locally. As you pilot inventory centrally, you can optimize policies globally. If appropriately done—using *multi-echelon inventory optimization* models[9]—it will result in massive savings that could never be achieved with local inventory policies. Moreover, even if you do not use advanced models, central inventory control will avoid shortage gaming. In the case of a shortage, you can enforce a fair-share allocation of available supply while ensuring that everyone is playing by the rules.

---

[9]   Aligning inventory policies across multiple echelons is called *Multi Echelon Inventory Optimization* (MEIO). Such global policies usually result in an 10-30% inventory reduction while keeping service levels constant. In my book *Inventory Optimization : Models and Simulation*, I introduce the *risk-horizon framework* which solves this optimization problem and in an elegant, straightforward way.

4.3.2 *External collaboration*

Aligning your supply chain with your clients and suppliers is often more challenging than ensuring internal alignment. Still, the rewards (better forecasts, lower costs, higher service levels) are usually worth the investment.

LEANER LOGISTICS TO PREVENT BULLWHIP

Before implementing a collaborative process with external companies, you can try to change your *own* logistics to promote leaner order patterns from your clients. You want to reduce order batching (*your clients order a lot at once*) and delayed orders (*your clients wait to make an order*). In practice, you want to set up your cost and pricing structure to promote frequent small orders from your clients. Similarly, making frequent small orders to your suppliers will help them capture your demand signal adequately.

COLLABORATION AND INFORMATION SHARING

We can roughly map four stages of collaboration between suppliers and clients (figure 4.7).

Figure 4.7 **Four stages of information sharing and collaboration**

1 *No information:* You do not have any special relationship with your clients. You simply receive orders, and that's basically it: clients won't share any extra data or information. You will ultimately suffer the bullwhip effect as you will have to rely on order forecasting while capturing a distorted demand signal (think about batch ordering, shortage gaming, delayed orders, and so on).

2 *Buying information:* In this second stage, you buy information from external data providers to access your clients' sell-out and inventory levels. Using this information *might* give you an edge when forecasting demand. But it won't be enough to unlock massive savings thanks to inventory optimization or planning alignment. Pay attention that using sell-out data to improve sell-in forecasts is not an easy task. Usually, statistical models struggle to capture the proper underlying relationships between sell-in, sell-outs, and inventory levels. Alternatively, you could try out two other techniques to leverage sell-out data:

a   As you do not know your client's inventory policies, you will have to double guess them using their historical average inventory levels. From there, you can forecast their sell-outs and guess your sell-in based on their current inventory levels. This process contains a lot of assumptions and is therefore not guaranteed to provide accurate sell-in forecasts.

b   Use machine learning models to forecast demand and feed them with sell-outs and inventory levels as extra features (chapter 15).

Moreover, information bought from external providers is usually partial and of low quality (and might be delayed) when it is not provided on an irrelevant aggregation level.

3   *Sharing information:* In this third stage, you will directly receive information from your clients: sell-outs, inventory levels, and, possibly, their inventory policies. The main difference with stage 2 is that you will usually get more data, more frequently, and of higher quality. More and better data usually results in better forecasts. The only remaining limitation is that you still can't align inventory policies with your clients.

4   *Collaboration:* In this last stage, on top of the information exchange, you will align your (supply/inventory) plans with your clients. Planning alignment will allow you to unlock massive savings thanks to *multi-echelon inventory optimization* and route optimization (if the supplier can plan the deliveries to many stores).

HOW TO BUILD COLLABORATION

There are three main approaches to build collaborative planning in a supplier-client relationship.

1   *Consignment:* The supplier owns and manages the inventory located at the client. Beyond the extra planning capabilities (and access to point-of-sales sales and inventory levels), this setup can be helpful if the supplier wants to promote risky products.

2   *Vendor Managed Inventory (VMI):* Similar to consignment, the only difference is that the client owns the inventory (but the supplier still manages it). In this situation, the client holds the financial risk, whereas the supplier leads supply planning and replenishments.

3   *Collaborative Planning Forecasting Replenishment (CPFR):* The most advanced stage of collaboration between supplier(s) and client(s). This framework enables end-to-end collaboration on supply and demand planning (usually through a common S&OP process). The supplier-client alignment

goes beyond supply quantities and stock targets: they can review pricing, marketing campaigns, promotions, etc. As many systems and processes need to be aligned, implementing CPFR is usually a significant undertaking requiring time, resources, and trusted partners. Henceforth, CPFR is mostly implemented by large supply chains (such as Walmart or Samsung). It is also more common in the food industry.

4.3.3 *Collaborating with your suppliers*

It's not all about sharing information and aligning planning with your clients. You can also collaborate with your suppliers. Sharing information (or aligning planning) will allow your suppliers to reduce their costs as they can optimize their planning. In turn, you should be in a better position to discuss discounts. Beyond cost reduction, you can also expect better information about supply and expected shortages, and more reliable lead times.

Summary

- The bullwhip effect (caused mainly by order forecasting, order batching, price fluctuations, shortage gaming, and variable lead times) will cause massive overstocks and shortages in supply chains.
- Bullwhip effect will ultimately result in extra costs and lower service levels for all stakeholders.
- Sharing demand and inventory data with your clients and suppliers will allow you to improve your forecasting accuracy and dampen the bullwhip effect. More information also usually means more stable lead times and fewer shortages.
- If your supplier-client relationship allows for planning alignment, you will also achieve massive savings thanks to multi-echelon inventory optimization.

Forecasting hierarchies

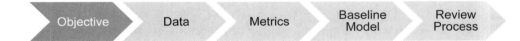

Objective → Data → Metrics → Baseline Model → Review Process

I have seen countless companies forecasting demand at irrelevant aggregation levels (material, geographical, or temporal) that do not match the information granularity required to make supply chain decisions. Many supply chains—especially manufacturers—typically rely on populating 18-month forecasts per country by monthly buckets. Should this be considered a best practice, or is it merely a by-default, overlooked choice?

In this chapter,[10] we will discuss forecasting hierarchies in detail. You will learn to assess your demand planning process's relevant material, geographical, and temporal aggregation levels (or dimensions).

---

[10] Note that the chapters follow a path meant to simplify your learning journey. They do not always strictly stick to the chronology of the demand-planning excellence framework.

5.1　*The three forecasting dimensions*

Demand forecasts are defined across three dimensions (or hierarchies): materiality, geography, and temporality.

- *Materiality:* You can forecast demand using different material levels: per SKU, product, segment, brand, and so on. As well as with different measuring metrics: units, value, weight, type of raw material required, ...
- *Geography:* You can forecast demand per country, region, market, channel, customer segment, warehouse, store, zip code, ...[11]
- *Temporality:* You can also use different time buckets (daily, weekly, monthly, quarterly, or even yearly).

We will discuss in section 5.3 why you could prefer one aggregation level over another. Finally, on top of these three dimensions, we will have to discuss the forecasting horizon:

- *Horizon:* How many periods forward do you need to forecast (one week, six months, two years)?

We will answer this question and discuss forecasting horizons in detail in chapter 6. For now, let's focus on materiality, geography, and temporality.

5.2　*Zooming in or out of forecasts*

We face numerous possibilities of forecasting aggregation levels across these three dimensions. For example, you could forecast demand per store, day, and product—or per month, country, and product family (figure 5.1).

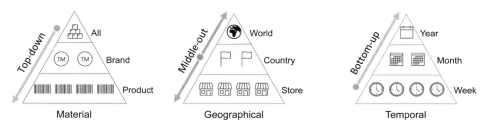

Figure 5.1　Aggregation and disaggregation techniques: top-down, middle-out, and bottom-up

---

[11] Some companies also add another dimension: *business profiles.* You can forecast your demand by sales channels, B2B vs. B2C, client segments, etc.

Let's illustrate these different granularity levels using a coffee shop as an example. To manage the shop, you could forecast demand at different aggregation levels:

- 27 lattes for tomorrow
- 5 gallons of milk for next week
- $4,800 worth of drinks for next month

Moreover, as illustrated in figure 5.1, you can easily disaggregate (zoom in) or aggregate (zoom out) any forecast using three techniques:

- *Bottom-up:* Aggregated forecasts are created by summing up granular downstream levels. For example, you can sum up the forecasts of each store in a country to get a forecast at the country level.
- *Top-down:* Detailed forecasts are created by disaggregating high-level forecasts (usually) using simple rules. For example, You can transform a monthly forecast into a daily one using a *flat split* (dividing the monthly forecast into daily buckets of equal amounts). Similarly, top-down forecasts can also be split using *historical splits* relying on historical weighted averages (or ratios). For example, you can spread a national forecast into its national stores based on their historical revenues. In practice, many forecasting tools will rely on techniques using historical averages to disaggregate top-down forecasts.
- *Middle-out:* This is an in-between situation: you can use a single forecast to generate a more aggregated view and a detailed version. For example, starting with a forecast per country, you can sum it up per geographical region and spread it by store.

In short, we can populate various different forecasts using different hierarchies. And we can navigate through different hierarchies using bottom-up, middle-out, and top-down approaches. Moreover, these approaches guarantee that forecasts reconcile at any granularity level. Later, in chapter 7, we will discuss another case where we allow variations along different granularities.

5.3   *How do you select the most appropriate aggregation level?*

All these *possible* hierarchies and aggregation techniques do not tell us what we need to do. Many practitioners have a high temptation to stick to the status quo: "We always forecasted demand per country per month."

But *you* need to challenge it by answering two questions:

- Which aggregation level should you focus on? In other words, which one is the most important?
  Are you really interested in a forecast per country per month?
- Which aggregation level should you use to create your forecast?
  Should you leverage daily data to generate your monthly forecast?

We could add a third one to these two: "Should we use multiple aggregation levels?" We will answer this later in chapter 7.

5.3.1 *Which aggregation level should you focus on?*

In a perfect dream world—where you have unlimited time, data, and computation power—you could compute all most possible granular forecasts (per hour, product, store, client, etc.). You could then reconcile these at any hierarchical level using bottom-up aggregation techniques. However, we must make choices in practice: data, reviewing time, and computation power are limited. Moreover, there is an accuracy glass ceiling that we can't break: we will never be able to make meaningful forecasts per product, client, store, and hour. Granular predictions are usually less accurate due to the increasingly high noise-to-signal ratio. *If you sold one item during the year and sold it in December, is it out of sheer luck or due to seasonality?* Looking at a higher level of aggregation will make these patterns easier to detect.

We must focus our time on a specific granularity level. But which one?

To answer this question, think about what decisions your supply chain colleagues will make based on your demand forecasts. Remember, a forecast is only relevant if it helps your supply chain make smart decisions (and take the right actions).

The idea is simple: because your supply chain makes decisions at specific hierarchical levels, you need to focus on forecasting demand to these particular aggregation levels.

Let's illustrate this with a few examples:

- Imagine you need to decide which products to ship from your plant to your regional warehouses. The best practice is to forecast demand per warehouse based on their geographical footprints (and not based on their actual historical shipments).

Pro note: Forecasting demand per warehouse

Using a warehouse's historical shipments to forecast demand is a bad practice: product availability and logistic constraints constrain historical shipments. Due to these constraints, close-by warehouses likely served part of the orders that couldn't be shipped directly from the main warehouse.

For example, suppose Warehouse A is out-of-stock. The incoming demand from its geographical footprint will be served from Warehouse B (the second closest to the customer). This will result in a misalignment between demand and shipments for Warehouses A and B.

Instead, you need to predict demand based on the geographical region that the warehouse usually serves. In other words, you need to forecast the demand that should be served from the warehouse, assuming there are no constraints. Tracking demand based on geography (for example, using zip codes) rather than outbound shipments is especially critical as warehouse footholds will change over time when new warehouses open or close.

- Many supply chains still forecast demand per country even though they have multiple warehouses serving different areas of the same country. This case is a clear discrepancy between the decisions that need to be made (*in which warehouse should we ship our products*) and the information used to make these (*we will sell that much in this country*). This too-common discrepancy will result in poor inventory allocation across warehouses.

TIP If you hear colleagues using techniques such as "we use a flat split to divide our monthly forecast in a weekly forecast" or "we use a flat split to spread our country-forecast per warehouse," you need to investigate if the forecasting process is aligned with the decisions.

- You should forecast per packaging if you need to set up your production process based on specific product packaging. When reviewing your forecast, you should then discuss what impacts the demand for each type of packaging: commercial events, promotions, etc.
- If you only have a single warehouse, you need to assess if forecasting per region or sales channel is worth the extra difficulty. A single forecast done at a global level might be enough to pilot your supply chain.
- Many other situations require granular forecasts. For example, if you have products with different growth rates, forecasting them separately might prove more accurate than using top-down techniques. You might also prefer granular forecasts if different forecast-items have different implications (type of subcomponents or raw material needed, price, etc.).

Moreover, note that different sales channels might require different forecasting aggregation levels. For example, suppose part of your business is make-to-order. This sales channel might require forecasting demand per subcomponents over the mid- or long-term. In contrast, your make-to-stock business will require a granular, short-term demand forecast.

5.3.2 **What granularity level should you use to create your forecast?**

This second question is often confusing for practitioners. Most think that once you know the granularity you are *interested* in, you will directly forecast demand using this granularity level. But that's not always optimal.

Before going further, we have to note that a forecast created using data at a specific granularity level will be (slightly) different from a forecast made from another level. For example, forecasting demand by looking at demand per week and channel might provide another number than running your model on monthly demand per market. This is because different historical signals and information will invariably result in different predictions.

Moreover, it is not because you are interested in forecasting demand at a specific granularity that you need to create your forecast directly at this granularity level. Indeed, you could leverage the information available at *another* granularity level. For example, as shown in figure 5.2, you could leverage daily information to make weekly forecasts—even if you are not directly interested in using daily forecasts.

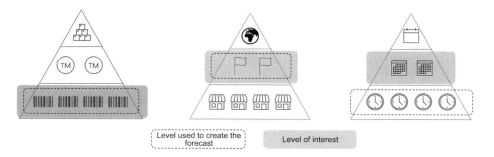

Figure 5.2   Level of interest vs. level used to create the forecast

Let's illustrate this using our ice cream truck. You replenish ice cream over the weekend and sell it during the week. Every weekend, you fill your ice cream from your supplier based on the demand forecast for the upcoming week. In this case, you want your weekly demand forecast to be accurate. But should you directly forecast demand by week? Maybe you could gather more insights using a daily forecast. For example, the school could be out on Monday. There might be a strike on Tuesday, bad weather on Wednesday (when kids typically buy more ice cream after school), and a game on Friday. By leveraging this information in a daily forecast, you'll achieve a much more accurate weekly forecast.

REVIEW PERIODICITY

You could also decide to update your forecasts more frequently. As new data becomes available, updating your forecasts *more* often might improve their accuracy. Updating them *too* often might create chaos as you overreact to demand changes and consume too many human resources for limited added value.

COMPARING APPROACHES

Nevertheless, leveraging granular data in a granular model won't *guarantee* more accurate forecasts. You will have to test both approaches, measure the results, and pick the best. In the earlier ice cream example, forecasting weekly demand leveraging daily data improved the forecasting accuracy. But we could imagine different scenarios where it wouldn't work. You will have to try multiple approaches and models to see what works best for your dataset.

Summary

- The first step of the path to demand planning excellence is to assess the forecasting granularity your supply chain is interested in.

- To do so, you need to understand your supply chain needs and requirements by investigating the decisions made based on the demand forecasts.

- Once you understand the main supply chain processes (sourcing, producing, delivering) and their underlying decisions, you can assess the optimal granularity level (materiality, geography, and temporality) that will provide the most useful and accurate forecasts to your colleagues.

- Then, based on the information and data at your disposal, you can assess the optimal information granularity to use when forecasting demand. In simple words, your supply chain might be interested in receiving forecasts on granularity A. Still, you can use granularity B to generate this forecast (using top-down, middle-out, and bottom-up techniques). Each level of aggregation will have strengths and challenges, especially where variation and uncertainty exist.

- As more data is captured or the nature of your business changes, you must prepare to try other configurations.

How long should the forecasting horizon be?

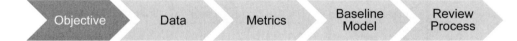

As a demand planner, the time you can dedicate to reviewing demand forecasts is limited. You need to focus your attention on a limited number of products and a limited forecasting horizon.[12] To put it simply, you cannot work on three-years-forward forecasts for every single product in your portfolio. You simply don't have the time. Instead, you need to focus your attention on the forecasting horizon that is the most useful for your supply chain.

How long should this high-focus forecasting horizon be?

As usual, you should answer this question by thinking about what your supply chain is trying to optimize and achieve—and the lead times involved with these decisions.

---

[12] The need to focus your attention on a few key elements—and how to do it—is central to this book; see more about this later in chapter 13.

Based on my experience, supply chains (especially manufacturers) often forecast demand up to 18 months forward (relying on forecasting models to populate all these predictions). But, as management tracks accuracy KPIs on a limited selection of lags (if not a single one), they implicitly (or explicitly) want planners to focus on a limited set of periods. Let's illustrate this with two statements I heard when discussing with clients:

- "We focus on forecasting M+2, and we only track KPIs for this lag as we need to plan production two months forward."
- "We focus on forecasting M+3 and M+12 (and only track KPIs for these two lags) as we need to have a view on mid- and long-term."

Lag

A lag denotes how many periods forward you are forecasting demand (as shown in figure 6.1). By convention, Lag 0 is the current period. For example, for a monthly forecast populated in January, Lag 0 denotes January, Lag 1 is February, Lag 2 is March, and so on.

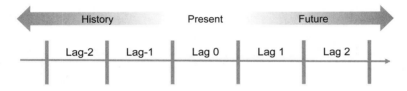

Figure 6.1 Forecasting lags

As you will see with an example, determining which lag(s) is the most important is often confusing. As a result, many (if not most) supply chains end up spending their time focusing on forecasting horizons that aren't aligned with their needs. It is time we change this and focus on the right horizon.

Let's imagine that you are a supply planner. Your main supplier is quoting you a lead time of three months, and you make monthly orders (figure 6.2).

Figure 6.2 Ordering process

Technically, you book your orders on the first day of the month (noted M1). And you receive the orders at the very beginning of a month. (Note that the received goods can't be used to fulfill the previous month's orders). You will make the next order on the first day of M1 and receive it on the first day of M4.

As a supply planner, you want your supply chain's demand planners to support you in this ordering process by providing helpful demand forecasts. On which lag(s) should they focus their time?

- A single month? Which one? M+1, M+2, M+3, M+4, or M+5?
- A range? M+1 to M+3, M+4, or M+5?

Take your time to think about this supply setup and answer the previous question before moving on.

I would focus on M1 to M5 (at least). Unfortunately, most planners are often confused by this question and would reply with either M+3 or M+4. To explain my answer, let's first look at the theory and then illustrate it with an example.

6.1   *Theory: Inventory optimization, lead times, and review periods*

Inventory optimization theory teaches us that *periodic* inventory replenishment policies[13] should be protected over a *risk-horizon*[14] equal to the supply (total) lead time plus the ordering review period.

As shown in figure 6.3, the risk-horizon of our earlier example is 4 months: 3 months of lead time plus a review period of one month.

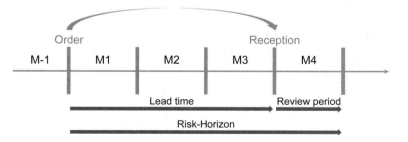

Figure 6.3   Lead time, review period and risk-horizon

---

[13] In practice, virtually all inventory policies are periodic. That is, supply and inventory processes follow a periodic ordering calendar. You cannot make an order at any point in time; instead, you will do an order once a day, a week, or a month. Unfortunately, academic textbooks and curriculums discuss continuous policies more often than periodic ones. This result in confused supply chain practitioners, especially because many software vendors also forget to include the review period in their models.

[14] Risk-horizon: Maximum amount of time you need to wait to receive an order (from your supplier). During this period, your inventory is at risk of being depleted. In periodic replenishment policies, we have risk-horizon = lead time + review period. I coined this concept in my book, *Inventory Optimization: Models and Simulations.*

This means that when making your order, you will need to consider the (forecasted) demand over the next four months to assess the appropriate quantity.

Based on this, the answer to the initial question ("which lag(s) should we focus on?") would be: "M+1 to M+4". This is counterintuitive for most planners who usually focus solely on M+3 or M+4 but not the cumulative M+1 to +4 forecast.

6.2   *Reconciling demand forecasting and supply planning*

Imagine the following orders and forecasts as highlighted in figure 6.4. When making your order (at the start of M1), you had an inventory level of 150 units.

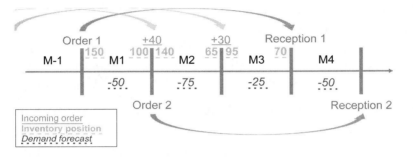

Figure 6.4   Orders and forecasts

You want to finish each month (*before* you receive a new order) with an inventory level of 100 units. (By defining inventory targets this way, it matches the definition of safety stocks.)

Example. At the end of M1, we expect to have an inventory of 100 units (= 150 − 50; starting position − expected demand). Then we'll receive our previous order of 40 units and reach 140 units to start M2. Based on your current forecasts, we predict that, by the end of M3, we will have an inventory of 70 pieces left. That's 30 pieces lower than our target of 100 units.

With a lead time of three months, Order 1 (that we are making now) won't arrive in time to impact the stock levels for the next three months. So, the only thing we can influence is M4 ending stock level.

As shown in figure 6.5, by ordering 80 pieces now, we'll ensure that the stock position at the end of M4 will be 100 units (starting = 70 + 80; consumption = 50; end position = 100).

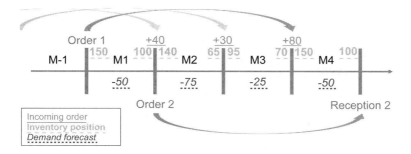

Figure 6.5 Sizing the current order to fit the inventory policy for M4

Looking at figure 6.4, we realize that changing any demand forecast from M1 to M4 will change the quantity we should order now.

Example. Suppose your demand planner updates M2 forecast by changing the expected demand from 75 to 100 pieces. In that case, you should also react by increasing your order by 25 units. (We will discuss the impact of lost sales and backorders in detail later in section 6.4.)

It means that any period from M1 to M4 is equally important to determine your order amount. This shows that freezing forecasts (even only freezing M1) is a bad practice that will result in less relevant orders. You can regularly update your short-term forecasts *even* if your supply plans are frozen. Do not confuse the *plan* (what you are going to do, buy, produce, move) and the *underlying information* (how much demand you predict you will face in the future). As shown in the previous example, updating short-term forecasts will help you plan midterm decisions better, even if you can't act in the short term.

6.3 *Looking further ahead*

Let's recap the story so far. We need to make monthly orders to our supplier, which quoted a three-month lead time. We realized that to decide how much to order now, we had to pay attention to the demand forecast for the coming four months.

Actually, this is not yet the whole picture.

6.3.1 *Optimal service level and risks*

The science of inventory optimization teaches us that we need to optimize service levels to balance profitability and risks. You need to find the optimal equilibrium between the risks and costs of over- and under-stocking products.

Let's imagine two simple (extreme) scenarios (as displayed in figure 6.6):

- *Scenario #1:* M5 expected demand is 0 pieces.
- *Scenario #2:* M5 expected demand is 1000 pieces.

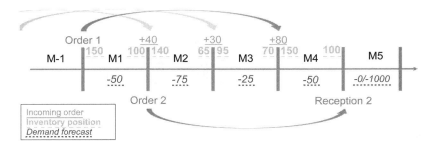

Figure 6.6   Scenarios 1 and 2 (M5)

We initially assumed that we wanted to finish M4 with a safety stock of 100 pieces. Obviously, if we do not expect any sales after M4 (Scenario 1), finishing M4 with an inventory of 100 pieces wouldn't be a wise decision. On the other hand, if we expect to sell a thousand pieces in M5 (Scenario 2), we could allow a bigger safety margin for M4 (because the risk of obsolete or long-term leftovers is low).

Many supply chains define safety stocks based on weekly coverages ("We want to keep three weeks of safety stock for our main products"). Therefore, the stock target at the end of M4 will be based on the M5 forecast.

6.3.2   *Collaboration with suppliers*

Improving forecasting accuracy beyond the *direct* risk-horizon might also be helpful. For example, by providing a long-term view to your suppliers (and other stakeholders), you can help them to reduce supply lead times, costs, and increase their service level. Sharing expected supply requirements with your suppliers could also be an opportunity to improve your overall relationship and start sharing more data, as discussed in chapter 4.[15]

6.4   *Going further: Lost sales vs. backorders*

Inventory policies with backorders (all *excess demand*[16] is kept until stock is available) differ from policies with lost sales (all excess demand is lost).

6.4.1   *Lost sales*

As customers (usually) cancel their orders when you are out of stock, you need to pay attention to any shortage that might happen over the risk-horizon. So, you need to have a detailed picture of what could happen during each month

---

[15] Pay attention to share your expected *supply requirements* with your suppliers and not your raw demand forecasts. You need to take into account your current inventory levels and inventory policies before communicating any supply plan to your supplier.

[16] Excess demand is defined as any demand that cannot be fulfilled directly from stock.

(on top of having a good forecast over the entire risk-horizon). See an illustration in figure 6.7.

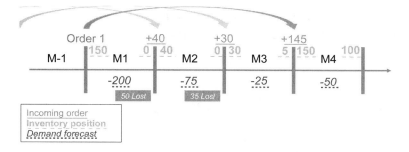

Figure 6.7   Lost sales: If M1 demand increases by 150 units (to 200 pieces), the impact on the order is only an increase of +65 units as the excess demand of M1 and M2 is lost.

Lost sales are common in B2C and FMCG (Fast Moving Consumer Goods) industries, making it particularly difficult for demand planners to estimate the actual demand (as discussed in chapter 3).

> **Pro Tip**
>
> In case of historical shortages, you will have to track unconstrained demand and not constrained sales (as discussed in chapter 3). Similarly, when looking at future forecasts, always keep in mind that you are forecasting unconstrained demand and not constrained sales. You should forecast demand *even* if you currently suffer a shortage or are about to. Do not forecast sales and stay out of the *Sales forecasting vicious circle* we discussed earlier in chapter 2.

6.4.2   *Backorders*

In case of inventory shortages, your clients will keep their orders open and wait for stock to be available again. (To put it differently, short-term shortages do not impact demand much.) If this applies to you, you should set up your planning systems to account for your current backlog when forecasting sales. Any forecast unconsumed due to supply constraints should automatically be carried over to the next period(s) (when supply is catching up again). If you forget to take into account this backlog, you will underestimate future sales (figure 6.8). (Note that I am making a difference between sales and demand: your period demand should be stable, whereas future sales will catch up with previously lost sales.)

In such a case, as shortages do not impact the total (expected) demand over the risk-horizon, you shouldn't focus on each individual period. Instead, make sure that the overall total forecast is correct.

In our earlier example, you should focus on the cumulative forecast from M1 to M4 rather than forecasting each month separately.

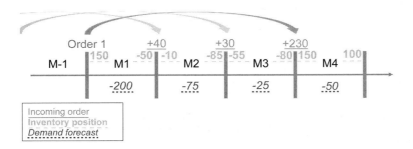

Figure 6.8   Backorders: If M1 demand increases by 150 units (to 200 pieces), the impact on the order is an increase of +150 units (80+150=230) because all excess demand is backordered.

6.4.3   *Hybrid*

In case of shortages, in most B2B supply chains, some clients will keep their orders open (or reorder later) while some will go to the competition (or use a replacement product). This will result in a mix of lost sales and backorders. In such a case, you will have to forecast each period accurately and have correct estimates over the whole risk-horizon.

Summary

- Focus on forecasting demand over the risk-horizon (total supply lead time plus review period) plus a few extra periods to cope with safety stock targets and collaborate with your suppliers.

- Do not focus your team efforts on just a few (or a single) periods as many supply chains do. This is a bad practice.

- Unfortunately, tracking and reporting accuracy over multiple periods will require a robust data management system (because you need to store numerous forecast versions). We will discuss forecasting metrics further in Part 2. Excel won't do the trick.

- Instead, you will have to use forecasting software or data management tools such as Python.[17]

---

[17] For example, these analyses can easily be performed using SKU Science—the forecasting online platform I cofounded in 2018.

Should we reconcile forecasts to align supply chains?

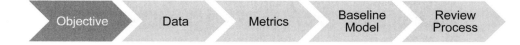

Objective → Data → Metrics → Baseline Model → Review Process

As we have discussed multiple times, supply chain management is about making decisions. As you orchestrate a supply chain, you want your teams to align their decisions. If marketing is preparing a product launch in Q2, you want your supply team to store enough inventory by the end of Q1.

To align teams along a supply chain, many advise using a single, shared forecast across all stakeholders (called a *one number forecast*). However, as we will discuss in this chapter, using different—but aligned!—forecasts (we call this *one number mindset*) might result in better decisions and more efficient forecasting processes.

7.1   *Forecasting granularities requirements*

In a supply chain, various teams and processes base their decisions on demand forecasts. As discussed in chapter 5, different stakeholders will have different requirements regarding forecasting horizon and material, geographical and temporal granularity (figure 7.1).[18]

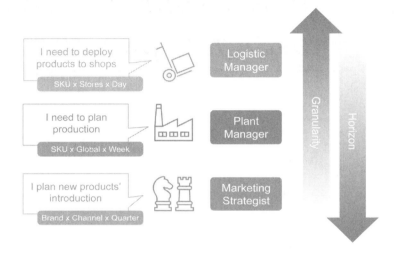

Figure 7.1   Supply chain roles and forecasting granularities and horizons

As illustrated in figure 7.1, a logistic manager might use the forecast to decide which shops to ship goods to in the next few days. In contrast, a plant manager must plan production for the next few weeks. A strategist marketer will use the same forecast to assess what product needs to be renewed in the next six to nine months. Finally, a finance manager will plan cash-flow based on a revenue forecast for the following quarters.

Usually, the teams using short-term forecasts will need granular information (per store, per product, per day), whereas teams using long-term forecasts will need aggregated information (such as per country or region, per product family, per month).

Supply chain management is about making decisions. So, how can we ensure all these teams are aligned when making their forecasts (and the resulting decisions/plans)?

---

[18] As discussed in the article *One-number forecasting* by Simon Clarke. Argon&Co, 2019, https://argonandco.com/us/news-insights/articles/one-number-forecasting-sandy-springs-atlanta-ga. Clarke, 2019.

7.2   *One number forecast*

To align the stakeholders along a supply chain, many practitioners[19] advocate using a reconciled (unified) forecast shared by everyone across a supply chain. This is known as a *one number forecast*. They hope that sharing a single unified forecast will force alignment across stakeholders. If different users need information presented at different granularity levels, we can mechanically align the forecasts using top-down, middle-out, and bottom-up approaches (which should be embedded in any modern forecasting software), as explained in chapter 5.

Still, this one number forecast approach will come with challenges.

- *Efficiency:* You will face a tedious recurrent alignment process. Can you imagine aligning the weekly forecasts of thousands of SKUs *every month* over the next 18 months?[20]
- *Optimality:* The optimal forecast (or model) at one material/temporal granularity level will not be optimal at another granularity. (We already discussed this effect in chapter 5, and we will illustrate it further in the next section.) One size can't fit all.
- *Alignment:* Using a *one number forecast* doesn't guarantee that all the teams within the supply chain are aligned. Bowman (2013) discusses an example where Nestle USA agrees on a single number forecast during their S&OP process. And yet, each department was still performing some internal cooking. For example, to plan production and supply, a manufacturer might need to forecast demand over the long-term per monthly buckets and type of raw materials (or subcomponents). In contrast, its logistic department will need to forecast demand coming from its distributors by day, leveraging information such as short-term promotions and shortages. Both forecasts will support different processes and might be slightly different.

One number forecast might help with alignment and clarity across a supply chain, but as we have seen, it has its cons as well. Let's discuss another framework (*one number mindset*) that allows slight forecast variations across the hierarchies.

---

[19] As discussed in Clarke (2019) and Bowman (2013).
[20] A stock keeping unit (SKU) refers to a specific material kept in a specific location. Two different pieces of the same SKU are indistinguishable.

7.3   *Different hierarchies . . . different optimal forecasts*

A significant issue of using unified forecasts is that a single forecast (or model) can't be optimal for all hierarchical levels.

Planners are often surprised to see that a forecast made at SKU level will differ from a prediction made at family level. This is normal, but frustrating! Forecasters know well that the *forecast of the sum is not the sum of the sub-forecasts*. In other words, a bottom-up forecast will not match one-to-one a forecast directly made at a high aggregation level.

Let's take a look with a detailed example as illustrated in figure 7.2. We want to forecast three different products (A, B, and C). We have demand history until period 23, and the forecasts start at period 24.[21]

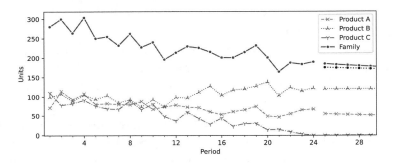

Figure 7.2   Top-down vs. bottom-up forecasts

To make the family-level forecast, we can use two different approaches:

- *Bottom-up:* We sum up the forecasts made for products A, B, and C. (See the dotted black forecast in figure 7.2.)
- *Direct:* We forecast directly the family-level time series. (See the blue plain forecast in figure 7.2.)

As you can see, both approaches result in different total forecasts. Beyond the math, let's discuss two business drivers behind this effect.

7.3.1   *Spot sales and stock clearances*

The sales of a product family can be reasonably stable over time at an aggregated level (figure 7.2 is a good example). Whereas, at SKU level, you will see many spot sales due to flash promotions, surplus stock clearance, specific one-time sales, or contracts. Those spot deals are often impossible to forecast

---

[21] These forecasts have all been generated using a double smoothing model. See my book, *Data Science for Supply Chain Forecasting,* for more details about this technique.

precisely by SKU. Forecasting models use historical demand to predict future sales. How could they expect stock clearances on SKUs that have not been sold for a long time?

An aggregate forecast (for example, expressed in value rather than units) could assume that some spot sales will take place. But you won't be able to use any top-down technique[22] to spread these spot sales by SKUs. For example, even if you know that you will do some stock clearance for a product family, you do not know which SKU your clients will buy precisely.

Moreover, as a demand planner, you should pay close attention so as not to include historical stock clearances when populating future forecasts. If not, you risk triggering new replenishments for dying items. This effect was famously experienced by Volvo and told by Professor Hau Lee. In the mid-1990s, Volvo found itself with too many green cars that were difficult to sell. Nevertheless, the sales and marketing department did their best to get rid of these cars thanks to promotions. On the other side of the supply chain, the manufacturing team saw a rise in green car sales. Unaware that their sales colleagues had to resort to massive discounts, they quickly decided to produce even more of them to match demand with supply.

7.3.2   *Product life-cycles*

(New) products come and go over time. As forecast engines mostly use historical demand to predict future sales, you cannot expect them to anticipate new SKUs' future introduction out of the blue. On the other end, forecast engines will spot any downward trend of a product nearing its end-of-life. This double effect will often bias long-term bottom-up forecasts: engines will predict end-of-life but will not include any replacement. On the other hand, if a product family is stable, top-down forecasts will not suffer from this effect.

In conclusion, even if you can easily come up with an 18-month forecast at family level, translating it to a SKU level might not be optimal. You do not know which SKUs will compose this family's total sales (even if you can predict the main products).

7.3.3   *Example: top-down vs. bottom up*

Imagine you are the planner responsible for forecasting demand for fruits at a supermarket. The assortment consists of tens of different fruits. Every month you sell around 10,000 fruits: mostly pears and apples, and a few pieces of the other less-known fruits.

---

[22] Top-down forecast: a forecast done at family level that is spread to SKU based on historical values. See chapter 5.

You can forecast these using two different approaches (see table 7.1):

- Bottom-up forecasting (disaggregated forecast). Using your statistical forecasting engine, you predict a monthly demand of 4,500 apples and 5,000 pears (for a total demand of 9,500 fruits).
- Top-down forecasting (aggregated forecast). The engine now predicts a total expected demand of 10,000 fruits.

Table 7.1   SKU Forecast vs. Scaled Forecast

Fruit	Demand	Bottom-up (Fruits → Family)		Top-down (Family → Fruits)	
		Forecast	Absolute Error	Forecast	Absolute Error
Apples	4,500	4,500	0	4,737	237
Pears	5,000	5,000	0	5,263	263
Kiwis	500	0	500	0	500
Total	**10,000**	**9,500**	**500**	**10,000**	**0**

As shown in table 7.1, the aggregated top-down forecast is more accurate if you measure accuracy at the family level. On the other side, the bottom-up forecast is more accurate if accuracy is measured per fruit. Yet, if we would scale this bottom-up forecast from 9,500 apples and pears forecast to a total of 10,000 units (as shown in Table 7.1), it would not result in any improvement—actually, the accuracy per SKU will even deteriorate.

In this example, the difference between the bottom-up forecast (9,500 units) and the top-down family forecast (10,000 units) is due to unexpected fruits that are usually not sold (such as Kiwis). These sporadic sales can't be predicted at a SKU level by an automated forecast engine. Yet a forecasting model can capture this at an aggregated level.

In short, you have no way to know which "less-known" fruit will be sold next month. So, scaling the forecast of apples and pears to 10,000 units will *destroy value* at the SKU level.

Advanced topics: Reconciling probabilistic forecasts

Working with probabilistic forecasts won't solve this reconciliation problem. It will make it worse because demand for different items is usually *not* independent. Some demand drivers will push demand for all fruits upward or downward (such as a massive promotion on another product in the store). On the other side, clients might choose to buy either one fruit *or* another. So that the probabilistic distribution at a higher level of aggregation will not be the sum of the lower-level demand distributions (see an example in table 7.2).

Table 7.2   Example of Probabilistic Forecasts Reconciliation

Quantiles	Forecast by		
	Apples	Pears	Apples & Pears
25%	2,000	2,000	5,000
50%	4,000	5,000	9,000
75%	7,000	9,500	15,000
95%	10,000	12,500	20,000

On the other hand, *point forecasts*—that is, single-value forecasts aiming at the average demand (in short, the typical forecasts we all use in supply chains)—are easily reconcilable at any aggregation level.

This effect is well-known to forecasters. In 2020, the M5 international forecasting competition—about forecasting Walmart sales at different aggregation levels (by products, product families, stores, and states)—asked to forecast specific demand distributions for each aggregation level.[23] By asking for different distributions per aggregation level, they acknowledged that product demand distributions shouldn't be reconciled with product families' demand distribution.

7.4   *One number mindset*

A new idea emerged next to the concept of one number forecast: *one number mindset*. Instead of forcing everyone's alignment on a single forecast, this construct proposes to align all stakeholders (supply and demand planners, finance, marketing) on a single mindset. As advised by Bowman (2013) and Wilson (2019), the idea is to share assumptions, data, and a clear vision of the future rather than force everyone to align on every SKU's forecast (and fit every stakeholder's requirements in a single forecast process). Each team should be aware of any information that could impact demand, such as pricing, marketing events, product introductions, competitors' actions, etc.

In practice:

- Every team should be required to use the same reconciled demand, pricing, and master data (as well as any other relevant information sources).

---

[23] See MOFC (2020).

A supply chain cannot allow two teams to use different historical figures to populate forecasts.[24]

- A formal process should be set up to share information about events impacting demand (such as price change, marketing events, product introductions, competitors' actions . . .). The S&OP process could be the right channel to share information across teams.

- Finally, forecasts done by various teams should be easily accessible to the other teams. To prevent any significant deviations from each other, all forecasts could be required to fluctuate within a specific (narrow) range. As discussed, small discrepancies are acceptable and natural. Still, any significant difference (anything higher than 5% at the global level) might result in a lack of alignment in the overall supply chain.

Each function will be aligned with this aligned mindset and shared data despite working with a different forecasting process (using different aggregation levels) and slightly different numbers.

Aligning teams thanks to a single mindset will allow every stakeholder to work on its required forecast granularity while enabling alignment on the main demand drivers (new product introduction, price changes, special events, and so on). This will leave more room for each team to define its own forecasting process using the most appropriate forecasting model, ultimately improving the overall forecasting quality. As explained by Clarke (2019), rather than influencing each other to achieve a single number forecast, teams will now have more time to discuss planning as they avoid reconciliation overload.

For example, a supply chain could have an S&OP process based on a country x month granularity. Nevertheless, another forecast could be made per warehouse per week to optimize the weekly deliveries from the global production plant to the local warehouses. Both forecasts would be generated using the same historical demand dataset but using different models and review processes. Moreover, demand planners will review short-term forecasts to make sure they stick within a reasonable range to the S&OP forecast. If not, planners can easily scale the short-term forecast based on the S&OP numbers. Finally, any major event discussed in the main S&OP meeting (such as price changes or special sales) should be used to fine-tune the short-term forecast.

---

[24] I could tell countless horrific stories of consultancy projects with clients providing me different demand and sales datasets depending on who was extracting and sending the data (everyone assuring me that *they* had the right data).

Summary

- A single united demand forecast (one number forecast) might provide a solid ground to align teams in a supply chain.

- If your supply chain needs to make different decisions on very different timescales (for example, *what to ship over the following days versus how much to buy over the next twelve months*), you might want to revert to a *one number mindset* where you align data and vision—but do not force forecast alignment.

Part 2

Measuring forecasting quality

In part 1, we defined our objectives: forecasting unconstrained demand on the appropriate horizon and granularity to support supply-chain decisions. In this second part, we will discuss forecasting quality. Simply put, we want to assess is a forecast is good or bad. We will start by introducing different forecasting KPIs in chapter 8 (Bias, MAE, MAPE, RMSE), then discussing their pros and cons in chapter 9 (Spoiler, MAPE is the worst). In chapter 10, we will answer a central question to demand planning: "What is a good level of forecast accuracy?" by using benchmarks. Finally, in chapter 11, we will extend our KPIs to assess the forecasting quality of a whole product portfolio using value-weighted metrics..

Forecasting metrics 8

Objective ▸ Data ▸ Metrics ▸ Baseline Model ▸ Review Process

Why is forecasting metrics important for practitioners and businesses? Because insightful metrics provide valuable (and actionable!) feedback on what can be done to improve both the forecast and overall business performance. Simply put, you can only improve what you can measure. So, choosing the right metrics should be the first step of any improvement journey.

Unfortunately, many practitioners struggle to decide which forecasting metrics to utilize. Or do not understand or use them properly. Choosing the best metric(s) to assess the quality of a forecasting process (or model) is anything but straightforward. And it will have a profound impact on the resulting forecasts and on the subsequent business decisions! Depending on the metric selected, you might promote biased forecasts, give too much importance to extreme values (chapter 9), overlook critical products (chapter 11), or focus on the wrong forecasting horizon (chapter 6).

Measuring forecast accuracy (or error) is not a simple task, because there is no one-size-fits-all indicator. Each indicator will avoid some pitfalls only to present others.

61

We will first discuss in this chapter how to compute forecasting KPIs. In chapter 9, we will discuss the pros and cons of each metric. We will finally identify a set of metrics that will be the best compromise to support (most) demand-planning processes.

8.1   *Accuracy and bias*

When discussing the quality of a forecast, the first distinction we have to make is the difference between the *accuracy* of a forecast and its *bias*. Unfortunately, both are often incorrectly interpreted, which can lead to poor forecasts and business decisions.

Accuracy

The accuracy of a forecast measures how much spread there is between the forecast and actuals. Accuracy gives an idea of the magnitude of the errors but not their overall direction.

Bias

Bias represents the overall direction of the errors. It measures if forecasts are, on average, too high (forecasts overshot demand) or too low (they undershot demand).

Figure 8.1 gives us a closer look at the differences between accuracy and bias.

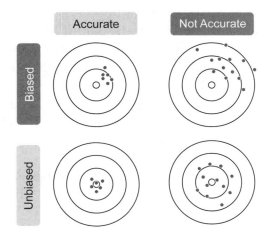

Figure 8.1   Forecasting accuracy and bias

As you can see in figure 8.1, we want an accurate, unbiased forecast. Unfortunately, we will often have to accept a compromise between these two dimensions. Even if it might sound counterintuitive, forecasts can be biased but accurate (dotted forecast in figure 8.2), or inaccurate but unbiased (dashed forecast in figure 8.2).

Before continuing your reading, answer the following two questions based on figure 8.2:

- Which of the two forecasts would you prefer for your supply chain?
- Which of the two forecasts would your current forecasting process (and KPIs) highlight as the best?

We will discuss how to compute accuracy and bias in the next sections. For now, assume that higher accuracy is better, and a bias close to 0 is better.

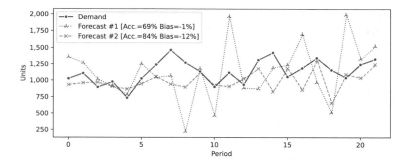

Figure 8.2 **Accurate but biased forecast (dashed) vs. inaccurate but unbiased forecast (dotted)**

Looking at these two forecasts, one could argue that Forecast 1 (inaccurate but not biased) might result in too much variation in the supply chain. On the other hand, Forecast 2 (accurate and biased) might result in lost sales and a poor signal to production. Note that biased forecasts (such as Forecast 2) might result from some teams intentionally making manual changes to the forecast (we will discuss how to solve this in chapter 16).

As this example shows, choosing the best forecast is sometimes not straightforward. You often have to make your choice based on multiple factors (Note that I didn't give a clear choice between Forecast 1 and 2.)

Let's analyze in the following sections multiple metrics to find a set of KPIs that would be aligned with our ultimate goal: Supporting our supply chain decisions by providing useful pieces of information.

> **Pro tip: Demand forecasting**
>
> Before tracking forecasting accuracy, you should be sure to compare forecasts with demand and not with sales. As discussed in chapter 2, you can think of demand as the orders placed by customers. If there is no stock to meet that demand, your sales might be lower for that period (we say that sales are *constrained*). In short, demand is what customers want. Sales is what you could achieve. We discussed in chapter 3 various techniques to unconstrained demand.

8.2   *Forecast error and bias*

We compute the forecast error as the forecast minus the demand. Mathematically, we note:

$$Error = e_t = f_t - d_t$$

The subletter t denotes the period. For example, we read `e_March = f_March - d_March` as "the forecast error in March is computed as March forecast minus March demand".

With this definition, the error will be positive when the forecast overshoots the demand; the error will be negative when the forecast undershoots demand.

You compute the overall forecasting bias by averaging the forecast error over multiple periods. Looking at bias over multiple periods is usually more relevant than for a single period. A consistent bias might be a clue that something is wrong with your forecast engine or with your forecasting process (we will discuss both aspects further in Parts 3 and 4). Bias can be calculated as follows:

$$Bias = \frac{1}{n} \sum e_t$$

> The symbol $\sum$ denotes a sum over multiple elements:
>
> $$Bias = \frac{1}{n} \sum e_t$$
>
> The equation reads as follows: "To compute the bias, we sum the error over multiple periods (for example, from January to December), then divide it by the number of periods." See table 8.1 for an example.

Table 8.1 Example with a Total Error of 7 Units over Four Periods *(Bias = 7/4 = 1.75)*

Period	Demand	Forecast	Error
January	10	15	5
February	5	12	7
March	8	5	-3
April	10	8	-2
Total	**33**	**40**	**7**

Let's now discuss how we interpret bias values.

8.2.1 Interpreting and scaling the bias

If you compute the bias based on the formula in the previous section, you will get an absolute value (for example, 1.75 units as in table 8.1). Imagine that you are investigating a product bias, and you get a result of 43 units. Is 43 units a good value? Without information about the product's average demand, you cannot answer this question. If the average demand per period is 10,000 units, a bias of only 43 is terrific. Still, it would be terrible if the average demand was 20 pieces. Therefore, a more relevant KPI is the *bias percentage* (that I note as Bias%). We can compute it by dividing the total error by the total demand, which is the same as dividing the average error by the average demand:

$$Bias\% = \frac{\sum e_t}{\sum d_t}$$

In our earlier example from table 8.1, the bias% would be computed as:

$$Bias\% = \frac{Total\ Error}{Total\ Demand} = \frac{7}{33} = 21.2\%$$

Note that it doesn't make much sense to compute the bias of a single product during a single period. Instead, you should either calculate the bias for a single item over many periods. Or compute it for multiple products at once (during one or multiple periods). Business-wise, it might be more relevant to look at bias across product families or products sharing the same resources (such as raw materials or production capacities). We will discuss how to track accuracy and bias for product portfolios in chapter 11. Moreover, as a general rule, avoid using percent errors when looking at a single period (we will discuss why in section 8.4 and later in chapter 9).

Let's now review how you can compute the bias yourself using Excel.

8.2.2   *Do it yourself*

> **Do it yourself**
>
> You can download the DIY Excel templates on my website https://supchains.com/
> demand-forecast-best-practices-book-resources/ (there is a blank and a corrected
> version). I highly encourage you to do these quick exercises to confirm your under-
> standing. The ability to compute forecasting KPIs on your own will give you a deeper
> understanding than a superficial reading.

In this dummy example, we have historical data (demand and forecasts) from
Period 1 to Period 21, as shown in figure 8.3. We want to assess historical accuracy and bias. For the sake of simplicity, we will not look at multiple lags (as
discussed in chapter 6). Instead, we will stick to analyzing the Lag 1 Forecast.
In plain English, we will look at the accuracy of the forecast made in Period 1
for Period 2, the forecast made in Period 2 for Period 3, and so on. Ideally, we
should do this analysis for all the relevant lags (see chapter 6 for more info).

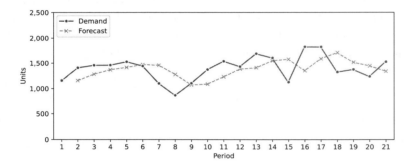

Figure 8.3   Historical demand and Lag 1 Forecast

You can quickly compute the forecast error as the forecast minus the demand.
In the example in figure 8.4, we calculate the forecast error in column C by
subtracting the demand in column A from the forecast in column B.

	A	B	C	D	E	F	G	H
1	Demand	Forecast	Error e=f-d					
2	1,159				Bias	-15.8	=AVERAGE(C3:C22)	
3	1,409	1,159	=B3-A3		Bias%	-1.1%	=F2/AVERAGE(A3:A22)	
4	1,458	1,284	- 174					
5	1,461	1,371	- 90					
6	1,527	1,416	- 111					

Figure 8.4   How to compute the bias in Excel

Once you have computed the forecast error in column C, you can calculate the bias by averaging it (see cell F2 and the formula in cell G2). You can also express the bias as a percentage by dividing it by the average demand.

> **Attention point**
>
> A common mistake (especially in Excel) is to divide the average error observed over a specific period by the average demand observed in another (more extensive) time range. Be sure to divide the average error by the average demand during the corresponding periods.

You should obtain something similar to figure 8.5 if you plot the demand, forecast, and error over time.

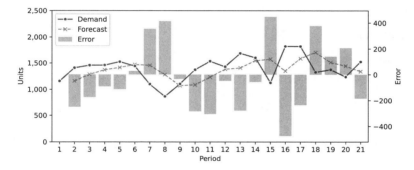

Figure 8.5 Demand, forecast, and forecast error over time

Now that you learned how to compute the bias on your own using Excel, we can conclude this section by discussing the limitations of using bias to assess forecasting quality.

8.2.3 Insights

Looking only at the bias won't be enough to evaluate your forecast quality. A positive error in one period can offset a negative error in another period. So, a forecast model can achieve very low bias and not be accurate at the same time (remember our discussion about Forecasts 1 and 2 in figure 8.3). A highly biased forecast indicates something is wrong in the model or the forecasting process (we will discuss potential causes in chapter 16).

> **Pro tip: How much bias should you expect?**
>
> In my experience (with statistical models and machine learning), forecasting engines usually result in a slightly negative bias when used to forecast product portfolios. This negative bias is primarily due to the products' lifecycles. Indeed, forecasting models can spot old products' declining sales trends. But they fail to predict new products' introductions on their own. Moreover, forecasting new products requires specific assumptions and insights (for example, about seasonality), creating further challenges in achieving good bias and accuracy.
>
> Chapter 10 will discuss a smarter way to assess if a forecast model is good or bad.
>
> Note that forecasting processes can often suffer positive bias due to management pressure. We will discuss this in chapter 16.

Now that we learned how to track forecasting bias, we can move on to assessing forecasting accuracy using the mean absolute error.

8.3   *Mean Absolute Error (MAE)*

The *Mean Absolute Error* (*MAE*) is a straightforward metric to measure forecast accuracy. As the name implies, it is the mean of the absolute error:

$$MAE = \frac{1}{n} \sum |e_t|$$

The symbol $|x|$ denotes the absolute value of value *x*. See an example in table 8.2.

Table 8.2   Example with a Total Absolute Error of 17 Units over Four Periods *MAE* = 17/4 = 4.25.

Period	Demand	Forecast	Error	Absolute Error
January	10	15	5	5
February	5	12	7	7
March	8	5	–3	3
April	10	8	–2	2
Total	**33**	**40**	**7**	**17**

Let's now dive into MAE by looking at its scaled version first; then you will learn how to compute it using Excel. Finally, we will quickly discuss some of its pros and cons.

8.3.1 Scaling the Mean Absolute Error

As for the bias, the MAE is usually expressed as an absolute number (for example, in table 8.2, we computed MAE as 4.25 units). If you are told that the MAE is 10 units for a particular product, you cannot know if this is a good or a bad forecast accuracy. If the average demand is 1000 units, achieving an MAE of 10 is astonishing. On the other hand, if the average demand is 1, an MAE of 10 is very poor accuracy.

Let's solve this by dividing MAE by the average demand to get a scaled percentage:

$$MAE\% = \frac{\sum |e_t|}{\sum d_t}$$

For example, in table 8.2, the MAE% would be:

$$MAE\% = \frac{Total\ absolute\ error}{Total\ demand} = \frac{17}{33} = 51.5\%$$

Note that we do not compute MAE% for every single period independently. It would result in computing MAPE, as we will do in the next section. Instead, we calculate MAE% at the end based on the overall total.

8.3.2 Do it yourself

Let's go back to our DIY case. You can compute the absolute forecast error in column C as |*forecast − demand*|. Then, you can compute the mean absolute error by averaging the absolute errors (see cell F2 and the formula in cell G2). You can also express the MAE as a percentage by dividing it by the average demand (see cells F3 and G3), as in figure 8.6.

	A	B	C	D	E	F	G	H
1	Demand	Forecast	|Error| =|f-d|					
2	1,159							
3	1,409	1,159	=ABS(B3-A3)		MAE	223.4 =AVERAGE(C3:C22)		
4	1,458	1,284	174		MAE%	15.8% =F2/AVERAGE(A3:A22)		
5	1,461	1,371	90					
6	1,527	1,416	111					

Figure 8.6   How to compute the mean absolute error (MAE) in Excel

Again, if you plot the demand, forecast, and absolute error over time, you should obtain a figure similar to figure 8.7.

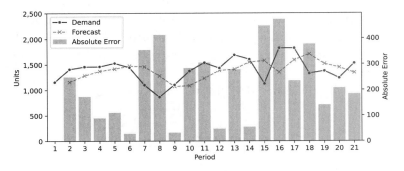

Figure 8.7   Demand, forecast, and absolute forecast error over time

Let's wrap things up by going over the insights to take away with regard to MAE.

8.3.3   *Insights*

MAE is a simple metric that is easy to explain to other team members and upper management. On top of that, you can easily express it as a percentage.

On the downside, minimizing MAE will often result in under forecasting. This is because minimizing the absolute error is similar to aiming at the median demand, which is usually lower than the average demand.[25]

Median

The median value of a dataset is the value that splits this dataset in half. This is not the same as the average. You can see in table 8.3 an illustration of the difference.

Table 8.3   Dataset with a Median of 4 and an Average of 13.2

Values	1	1	2	3	4	4	5	6	6	100

You have now learned to use MAE and its pros and cons. Next, let's move on to MAPE, a metric often confused with it.

---

[25] The proof is beyond the scope of this book. See my previous book, *Data Science for Supply Chain Forecasting,* for a detailed explanation.

8.4 Mean Absolute Percentage Error (MAPE)

The Mean Absolute Percentage Error (or MAPE) is one of the most commonly used metrics to measure forecast accuracy. Despite being a poor accuracy indicator—if not the most flawed—as you will see in the following section.

MAPE is computed as the average of the individual absolute errors divided by the demand (each period is divided separately). To put it simply, it is the average of the absolute percentage errors (APE):

$$APE = \frac{|e_t|}{d_t}$$

$$MAPE = \frac{1}{n} \sum \frac{|e_t|}{d_t}$$

Table 8.4 Example with a Mean Absolute Percentage Error (MAPE) of 61.875% = 1/4 (50% + 140% + 37.5% + 20%).

Period	Demand	Forecast	Error	Absolute Error	APE (Absolute Percentage Error)
January	10	15	5	5	50%
February	5	12	7	7	140%
March	8	5	−3	3	37.5%
April	10	8	−2	2	20%
Total	**33**	**40**	**7**	**17**	**61.9%**

8.4.1 Do it yourself

Do it yourself

Remember, you can download the DIY Excel templates on my website https://sup-chains.com/demand-forecast-best-practices-book-resources/.

You can compute the Absolute Percentage Errors (APE) in column C using the formula `abs(f-d)/d`. Then, you can compute the Mean Absolute Percentage Error (MAPE) by averaging all the percentage errors absolute errors (see cell F2 and the formula in cell G2) in figures 8.8 and 8.9.

	A	B	C	D	E	F	G	H
1	Demand	Forecast	APE =|f-d|/d					
2	1,159							
3	1,409	1,159	=ABS(B3-A3)/A3		MAPE	16.9%	=AVERAGE(C3:C22)	
4	1,458	1,284	12%					
5	1,461	1,371	6%					
6	1,527	1,416	7%					
7	1,443	1,472	2%					
8	1,102	1,457	32%					
9	866	1,280	48%					

Figure 8.8   How to compute the Mean Absolute Error (MAE) in Excel

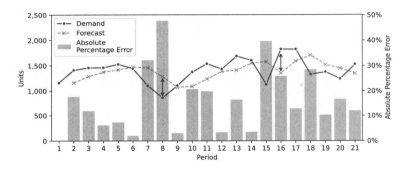

Figure 8.9   Demand, forecast, and absolute percentage error

Again, now that you know how to compute MAPE (and the differences compared to MAE), let's take some time to review the pros and cons of MAPE.

8.4.2   Insights

As you can see in the Excel table 8.4, MAPE divides *each error individually* by the corresponding demand—that's why this metric is so flawed. These individual divisions result in a skewed error weighting: high errors during low-demand periods will significantly impact MAPE (as the error is divided by a low value). As a consequence, if you want to minimize MAPE, you should stick to conservative forecast values to avoid committing high errors during low-demand periods.

In figure 8.9, you can observe that the percentage error is higher in Period 8 than in Period 16. Whereas Period 16 suffers a bigger absolute forecast error (for reference, both arrows in figure 8.9 have the same length).

You can see this from another point of view: an extremely low forecast (such as 0) can only result in a maximum percentage error of 100%, whereas too-high forecasts will not be capped to a specific percentage error. Due to this, optimizing MAPE will result in a strange forecast that will most likely under-shoot the demand.

We will discuss the pros and cons of each metric further in chapter 9. As you will see, MAPE only suffers drawbacks. Just avoid it!

Attention point

Many practitioners use the MAE% formula and call it MAPE. This can cause a lot of confusion. When discussing forecast error with someone, I advise you to explicitly specify how you compute the forecast error to be sure to compare apples with apples.

8.5 Root Mean Square Error (RMSE)

The Root Mean Square Error (RMSE) is computed as the square root of the average squared forecast error:

$$RMSE = \sqrt{\frac{1}{n} \sum e_t^2}$$

If you happen to forget the formula, you can use the metric's name (root mean square error) as a cooking recipe to compute it (table 8.5).

Table 8.5 Example with a Root Mean Squared Error (RMSE) of 4.66 = $\sqrt{(87/4)}$

Period	Demand	Forecast	Error	Squared Error
January	10	15	5	25
February	5	12	7	49
March	8	5	−3	9
April	10	8	−2	4
Total	**33**	**40**	**7**	**87**

8.5.1 Scaling RMSE

Again, RMSE is expressed as an absolute number and is not scaled to the demand. Just as for bias and MAE, you can divide it by the average demand to express it as a percentage:

$$RMSE\% = \frac{\sqrt{\frac{1}{n} \sum e_t^2}}{\frac{1}{n} \sum d_t}$$

In our earlier example (Table 8.5), we would compute RMSE% as:

$$RMSE\% = \frac{RMSE}{Average\ Demand} = \frac{4.66}{33/4} = 56.5\%$$

8.5.2   *Do it yourself*

You can compute the squared error in column C using the formula `(f-d)^2`. Then, you can compute the root mean squared error (RMSE) by taking the squaring root of the averaged squared errors (see cell F2 and the formula in cell G2) as in figure 8.10.

	A	B	C	D	E	F	G	H
1	Demand	Forecast	Error^2 =(f-d)^2					
2	1,159							
3	1,409	1,159	=(B3-A3)^2		RMSE	264.3	=SQRT(AVERAGE(C3:C22))	
4	1,458	1,284	30,276		RMSE%	18.7%	=F2/AVERAGE(A3:A22)	
5	1,461	1,371	8,100					
6	1,527	1,416	12,321					

Figure 8.10   How to compute the root mean squared error (RMSE) in Excel

It doesn't make sense to compute the RMSE period by period. It would be the same as computing the absolute error. Instead, you can plot the squared error as in figure 8.11.

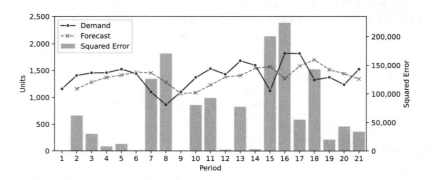

Figure 8.11   Demand, forecast, and squared error

8.5.3   *Insights*

The Root Mean Square Error (RMSE) can be challenging to interpret (and explain). It is defined as *the square root of the average squared forecast error.*

Nevertheless, RMSE can be very helpful for three main reasons.

First, it allocates more importance to the most significant forecast errors. As shown in figure 8.11, RMSE is nearly only penalizing us for the errors committed in periods 7, 8, 15, 16, and 18. In contrast, many periods are virtually insignificant (6, 9, 12, and 14). Allocating more weight to the biggest errors is useful because the impact of forecast errors on supply chains is not linear: massive errors have huge impacts (lost sales, dead stocks), whereas small errors have nearly no impact.

Second, RMSE is actually related to most inventory optimization formulas when it comes to computing the required amount of safety stocks.[26]

Moreover, RMSE is an unbiased metric: a good score on RMSE often correlates with an unbiased forecast.[27] We will discuss the pro and cons of forecasting metrics further in chapter 9.

8.6 Case study – Part 1

To put these forecasting KPIs into context, let's do a case study.

You are a demand planner overseeing a product. You have nearly two years of demand history, and you need to pick the best forecast among three forecasts.

You can see these three forecasts in figure 8.12 and the detailed data in table 8.6. (These are dummy, flat forecasts created for the purpose of this exercise.)

Before computing any metric, look at both and pick your favorite forecast.

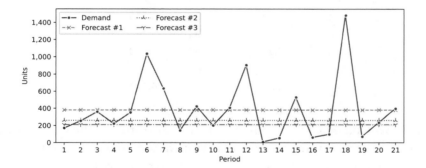

Figure 8.12   Demand and forecasts

---

[26] As usual, if you want to learn more about inventory optimization, see my previous book *Inventory Optimization: Models and Simulations*.

[27] See my previous book *Data Science for Supply Chain Forecasting* for a detailed explanation on how optimizing RMSE theoretically results in no bias.

In table form, they appear as follows.

Table 8.6   Demand and Forecasts

Period	Demand	Forecast #1	Forecast #2	Forecast #3
1	170	380	260	210
2	254	380	260	210
3	360	380	260	210
4	221	380	260	210
5	351	380	260	210
6	1034	380	260	210
7	632	380	260	210
8	142	380	260	210
9	421	380	260	210
10	200	380	260	210
11	405	380	260	210
12	904	380	260	210
13	8	380	260	210
14	52	380	260	210
15	528	380	260	210
16	60	380	260	210
17	97	380	260	210
18	1482	380	260	210
19	70	380	260	210
20	233	380	260	210
21	395	380	260	210
Total	**8,019**	**7,980**	**5,460**	**4,410**

Now that you have a favorite forecast, let's investigate the forecasting metrics. You can see them in table 8.7. If you want to deepen your understanding of forecasting metrics, I would advise you to compute these metrics yourself using the DIY templates on my website https://supchains.com/demand-forecast-best-practices-book-resources/.

Table 8.7   Forecasting KPIs for Forecasts 1, 2, and 3

Forecast	Bias	MAE	MAPE	RMSE
1	**−0.5%**	68.4%	352.9%	**94.4%**
2	−31.9%	**65.7%**	239.1%	99.6%
3	−47.6%	67.6%	**187.1%**	105.7%

Looking at these metrics, did your opinion about the three forecasts change? Which one is your favorite now? How is it better than the other two? Which KPI did you use to support your conclusion (if any)? I will answer these questions at the end of chapter 9.

We will continue to discuss forecasting KPIs in the following chapters, highlighting each metric pros and cons based on different cases.

Summary

- To track the quality of a forecast you have to measure both its bias and accuracy.
- Various forecasting KPIs can be used to track accuracy (MAE, MAPE, RMSE, among others).
- Forecasting KPIs have different pros and cons, we will discuss these further in Chapter 9.

Choosing the best forecasting KPI

| Objective | Data | Metrics | Baseline Model | Review Process |

In chapter 8, you learned how to compute various forecasting KPIs (Bias, MAE, MAPE, and RMSE—see table 9.1 for a recap). Unfortunately, as highlighted in the case study in section 9.4, depending on the KPI you pick, you might end up choosing different forecasts. (Remember, the objective of demand forecasting is to provide valuable information to the other teams in the supply chain so they can make appropriate decisions.)

Table 9.1 Forecasting Metrics

Metric	Formula	
Bias	$= \frac{1}{n} \sum e$	=average(error)
MAE	$= \frac{1}{n} \sum |e|$	=average(|error|)
MAE%	$= \dfrac{\sum |e|}{\sum d}$	=sum(|error|)/sum(demand)
MAPE	$= \frac{1}{n} \sum \frac{|e|}{d}$	=average(|error|/demand)
RMSE	$= \sqrt{\frac{1}{n} \sum e^2}$	=sqrt(average([forecast-demand]²))

In this chapter, we will further analyze these metrics' pros and cons using two specific scenarios: extreme demand patterns (with outliers) and products with intermittent (sporadic) demand. Finally, we will conclude this chapter by selecting a combination of metrics that will provide a (very) good tradeoff between simplicity, accuracy, bias, and outlier sensitivity.

9.1 *Extreme demand patterns*

In the case of highly variable, sporadic demand (or the presence of outliers), RMSE might overreact to a few forecast errors as RMSE emphasizes the most significant errors (RMSE looks at *squared* errors). As you can see in figure 9.1, adding an outlier to a dataset will greatly impact RMSE.

$$RMSE = \sqrt{\frac{1}{n} \sum e_t^2}$$

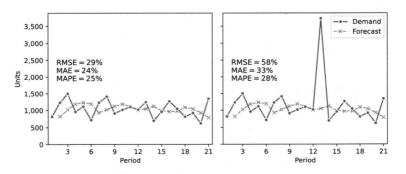

Figure 9.1 Historical demand with and without outlier (Period 13)

On the other extreme, extreme demand values will barely impact MAPE. This is because MAPE computes percentage errors by dividing each error by the corresponding demand. So, even in case of extreme demand, the maximum percentage error during one period is capped to 100%:

$$MAPE = \frac{1}{n} \sum \frac{|e_t|}{d_t}$$

MAE (or its percentage version) provides a much better compromise here: it is impacted by extreme values. But not too much.

9.2   *Intermittent demand*

Most supply chains deal with intermittent demand patterns for at least a few of their products—if not most of them.

See an example of such an intermittent demand pattern in figure 9.2. Most of the time, there is no demand for this product that is usually only sold once every three months. Forecast 2 only consists of forecasting zero demand over and over. This forecast won't be helpful for any supply chain decision-maker. (Remember, that's the main objective of our forecast: help other teams make smart decisions.)

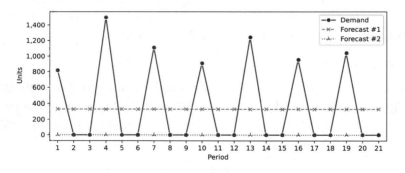

Figure 9.2   Intermittent demand pattern

You can see the corresponding forecasting KPIs in table 9.2.

Table 9.2   Forecasting Metrics for Intermittent Demand

Metric	Forecast 1	Forecast 2
Bias	−8.6%	−100.0%
MAE	130.5%	100.0%
RMSE	145.7%	176.5%
MAPE	inf	inf

Yet, Forecast 2 achieves a better MAE%. This is because MAE is minimized when the forecast aims at the median demand.[28] And in the case of intermittent demand, the median value is 0 (in other words, most of the time, you don't have any demand for your product).

See that MAPE is not defined when your historical demand data includes zeroes. Remember, MAPE divides each error by the corresponding demand value. So, in the case of zero demand, the relative error is then undefined.

On the other hand, in this example with intermittent demand, using RMSE as a leading metric would result in a much better, unbiased forecast.

9.3   *The best forecasting KPI*

You can see, in table 9.3, a recap of the pros and cons of each forecasting metric.

Table 9.3   **Recap of Forecasting Metrics' Pros and Cons**

Metric	Simple	Not Biased	Error Weighting	Sensitivity to outliers	Formula
MAE	☑	✘	✘	☑	$= \frac{1}{n}\sum |e|$
MAPE	☑	✺	✘	✘	$= \frac{1}{n}\sum \frac{|e|}{d}$
RMSE	✘	☑	☑	✘	$= \sqrt{\frac{1}{n}\sum e^2}$

Remember that MAE follows a uniform error weighting (each error unit is equally important). MAPE allocates more importance to periods with low demand, and RMSE will give more importance to high periods.

As we can see, no KPI is perfect. Yet, we must use a quantitative metric to evaluate forecasts. Which one should we choose?

Instead of looking for *the one perfect KPI*, we can use a combination of metrics to assess the quality of a forecast. I advise looking at both MAE and bias to evaluate a forecast. This combination provides the best tradeoff between simplicity and overall robustness as it properly gauges bias and accuracy while avoiding most pitfalls (see table 9.4).

---

[28] The detailed explanation of this effect is beyond the scope of this book. For more information see my other book *Data Science for Supply Chain Forecasting*.

In practice, if you want to assess a forecast quality using a single metric you can compute a "combined score" by summing its MAE and the absolute bias:

$$Score = MAE + |Bias|$$

Pay attention that if you forget to take the absolute value of the bias, you will reward under-forecasting.

Table 9.4   Recap of Pros and Cons

Metric	Simple	Not Biased	Error Weighting	Sensitivity to outliers
MAE & Bias	✓	✓	✗	✓

You can also compute a percentage version:

$$Score\% = MAE\% + |Bias\%|$$

Using this score will prove practical to compare quantitatively different forecasts easily. But it might be confusing for non-experts. If you want to discuss forecasting quality with management, I advise presenting separately MAE and Bias rather than in a single percentage.

Using this score is a best practice when assessing the accuracy of a single product. In chapter 11, we will build on this score and discuss how to evaluate forecasting quality over a whole product portfolio.

Pro Tip: Forecasting KPIs and lags

As discussed in chapter 6, we should focus our forecasting efforts on the whole relevant forecasting horizon. Not just on a single lag. So, when measuring accuracy, do not forget to track it for multiple lags. Analysts might want to look at each lag's accuracy, bias, or score. But management might find it more helpful to look at an aggregated number or scorecard.

9.4   Case study – Part 2

Let's continue with our case study from chapter 8. We had to pick our favorite forecast among the three, as shown in figure 9.3.

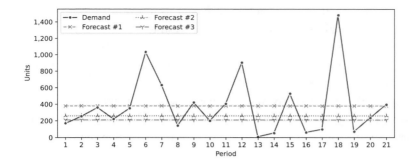

Figure 9.3 Demand and forecasts

You computed various KPIs for these forecasts in chapter 8 (as shown in table 9.5). It wasn't clear what forecast was best to choose over the other. Indeed, each forecast minimize another metric (see table 9.5). For example, by selecting Forecast 1, you could minimize RMSE and bias, but this would result in the worst MAE and MAPE.

If we score each forecast based on the combination of MAE and abs(Bias), we get a clear winner: Forecast 1 with a combined score of 68.9%. This forecast will provide the best compromise between accuracy and bias, ultimately delivering the most helpful piece of information to the other teams in the supply chain.

Table 9.5 Forecast 1 Provides the Best Compromise Between Accuracy and Bias with a Combined Score of 94.9%

Forecast	Bias	MAE	MAPE	RMSE	Score MAE + |Bias|
1	**−0.5%**	68.4%	352.9%	**94.4%**	**68.9%**
2	−31.9%	**65.7%**	239.1%	99.6%	97.6%
3	−47.6%	67.6%	**187.1%**	105.7%	115.2%

Moreover, Forecasts 2 and 3 are massively biased. Using one of these two will most likely result in painful shortages. Based on my experience, any forecast engine (or process) resulting in consistent bias (anything beyond 5%) should be considered suspicious. Forecasts 2 and 3 are way beyond this range as they display massive biases (−31.9% and −47.6%, respectively). Such numbers are a clear symptom of something wrong with the model (chapters 14 and 15) or the process (chapter 16). Moreover, some supply chains set safety stocks targets based on days of coverage. This will result in massive shortages in case of under-forecasting.

You can communicate this conclusion easily to management without any reference to a score metric ("We computed the sum of MAE and the absolute bias and expressed it as a percentage score"). Instead, what about: "Forecast 1 represents the best tradeoff between accuracy and bias as both are important to run our supply chain."

Note that in this case study we do not discuss forecasting lags. To do an in-depth analysis, you should compute these metrics for each lag over the whole relevant forecasting horizon (chapter 6). Then, select the best overall forecast based on all the results.

We will discuss more insights in the following two chapters:

- *Chapter 10:* How to assess what is a good (or poor) forecasting accuracy.
- *Chapter 11:* How to scale our metrics when we deal with a portfolio of products.

Summary

- To properly assess the quality of forecasting models or processes, track both MAE and bias. Looking at these two metrics is a (very) good compromise, enabling you to track accuracy and bias while avoiding most pitfalls.
- In any case, avoid using MAPE. Unfortunately, many practitioners still use it as a forecasting metric. Still, MAPE is a highly skewed indicator leading to under-forecasting.

What is a good forecast error?

Objective → Data → **Metrics** → Baseline Model → Review Process

When teaching students or training professionals on forecasting KPIs, I like to repeat over and over the same question: "How do you know if a forecast is good enough?" Take a minute to think about this question (you can directly refer to your own demand planning process).

Usually, students and professionals reply along these lines:

- *"We compare this year's accuracy against what we achieved last year."*
  But what if last year was especially good or bad? For example, the accuracy you achieved forecasting March 2021 is likely much better than the one achieved in March 2020, which was probably dramatically low due to Covid lockdowns.

- *"Anything lower than our accuracy target is acceptable."*
  This is a chicken and egg problem: how do we set the accuracy target in the first place?

- *"We compare our forecast to another forecast and see if we can beat it."*
  This is not a bad idea, but against which forecast (tool or model) should you compare yourself?
- *"This forecast looks correct (as it follows trend and seasonality), so it should be good."*
  Visually assessing forecasts might provide you with some insights, but it is not a standardized practice to evaluate their quality. And it is not scalable. You cannot visually assess thousands of forecasts.

Some professionals also mention using industry benchmarks. We will discuss them (and see why this is a bad practice) in chapter 12. Others advise using COV (demand coefficient of variation). This is also a bad practice, as we will discuss later in this chapter.

Let's discuss forecasting quality further using an example. Figure 10.1 shows the historical demand of a product along with a forecast populated by a statistical model. This forecast achieved a historical MAE of 36.1%. Should it be considered accurate? Would you be satisfied if your forecasting tool showed you a forecast error of 36.1% and a bias of 1.6%?

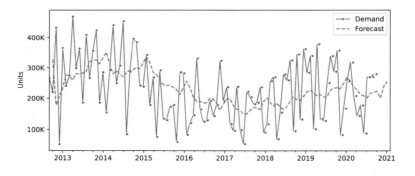

Figure 10.1   The dashed forecast achieved an MAE of 36.1% and a bias of 1.6% (manufacturer in the pharma industry)

Answering this question without further information is impossible as it is exceedingly difficult to estimate *a priori* a reasonable forecast error for a particular dataset. Indeed, the accuracy of a model depends on the demand's inner complexity and random nature. For example, if you express accuracy and bias in relative terms, forecasting the number of smartphones sold in a country per month is much easier than predicting the sales of a specific phone model, at a particular store, on a specific day. Moreover, different industries will benefit from different insights. For example, thanks to collaborative planning, some manufacturers can achieve outstanding accuracy (chapter 16). On the other hand, the fashion industry will struggle to forecast demand accurately as products have short shelf lives and demand is spread out between so many sizes, colors, and styles.

10.1 Benchmarking

Yet, there is a simple way to assess a dataset's complexity and the quality of any forecast made on it. To know if the accuracy achieved by a forecasting model on a given time series is good or bad, you must compare it against the accuracy achieved by a *benchmark*: a simple forecasting model. The remainder of this section will consider the question: *which forecasting benchmark should we use?*

10.1.1 Naïve forecasts

A *naïve forecast* is the simplest forecast model: it always predicts the last available observation. For example, suppose you sold 10 pieces today. In that case, you will forecast a demand of ten pieces per day (no matter how much you sold yesterday and the days before). You can see an example in figure 10.2.

Using naïve forecasts as benchmarks used to be considered as a best practice. And many practitioners and software vendors still recommend using them. See figure 10.2 for an illustration.

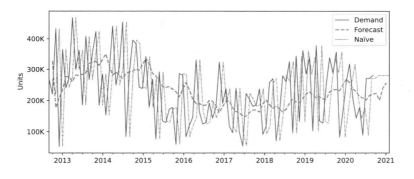

Figure 10.2 Forecast vs. naïve benchmark; see metrics in table 10.1

I do not advise using naïve forecasts as benchmarks because they are too inaccurate (see results in table 10.1). They will provide poor results easily beatable by any other forecasting technique. Because beating a naïve forecast is too easy, achieving a better forecast accuracy than this benchmark shouldn't be considered satisfactory for a model. Do not be fooled by anyone (consultants or software vendors) proclaiming to beat such a benchmark as a best practice and a win.

Table 10.1 Forecast Versus Benchmarks

Model	MAE%	Bias%	Score MAE + |Bias|
Forecast	37.0%	1.1%	38.1%
Naïve	50.7%	−0.1%	51.8%
MA6	36.3%	0.5%	36.8%

10.1.2 *Moving average*

A more competitive contender for a benchmark is a moving average. A moving average is straightforward to compute and will provide much better results than a naïve forecast. Usually, averaging the last 3 to 6 periods achieves the best results (figure 10.3).

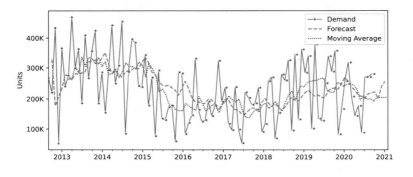

Figure 10.3   Forecast vs. benchmark; see metrics in table 10.2.

When comparing your forecasts to benchmarks, pay attention to following points:

- Try out a few different moving averages to select the best benchmark. This way, you will be sure not to use an artificially poor benchmark. And, in the case your baseline model doesn't beat the selected benchmark, well, you just found your new model.
- When comparing your forecasts with benchmarks, pay attention to comparing them based on the same lag. For example, a forecast made at M-3, should be compared with a moving average based on the demand from three months ago.
- Do not compare your model against a benchmark over a historical period that was used to optimize your model. For example, suppose you select a

model among 15 different possibilities based on whichever achieved the best results in 2022 (that's how most modern forecasting software work). In that case, you can expect that this winner will beat the benchmark in 2022. But this model might fail to deliver good results in 2023. This effect is called overfitting: the model worked well on historical data but failed to replicate its results on future data. For more information about overfitting, see my previous book, *Data Science for Supply Chain.*

- Comparing your model against a benchmark shouldn't be a one-off exercise. Keep on tracking both over time. We will discuss this further in chapter 12.

10.1.3 Seasonal benchmarks

If you face seasonal demand, you can try using *seasonal* benchmarks. Instead of using the previous period(s) to forecast the next one, you use the same-period(s)-last-season(s) demand to forecast each new period. These forecasts are then called either *seasonal naïve forecasts* (only using information from the previous seasonal cycle) or *seasonal moving averages* (averaging multiple cycles).

For example, as shown in figure 10.4 and table 10.2, if you sell a product with a daily seasonality, you can use a seasonal moving average of the last three weeks as a forecasting benchmark. This seasonal benchmark will forecast Mondays' demand as the average of the last three Mondays.

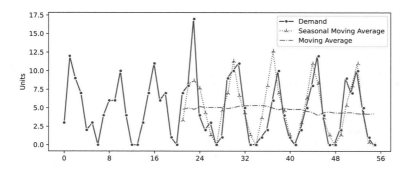

Figure 10.4 Seasonal moving average vs. moving average for seasonal products

As shown in table 10.2, the seasonal benchmark is much more accurate than a regular moving average forecasting Mondays as the previous three weeks' demand average (including Tuesdays, Wednesdays, and so on).

Table 10.2 KPI Comparison

Benchmark	Bias	MAE	RMSE	Score MAE + |Bias|
Seasonal moving average	2.6%	42.5%	59.9%	45.1%
Moving average	0.6%	77.6%	91.5%	78.2%

As we have discussed, using simple forecasting models as benchmarks will give you a free, straightforward way to compare your forecasting accuracy against a fair contender.

10.2 *Why tracking demand coefficient of variation is not recommended*

Note to the reader

The sole objective of this section is to explain why tracking demand coefficient of variation (COV) is a bad practice. If you know this already or simply do not use COV, feel free to skip to the Summary.

Many supply chain practitioners and thought leaders recommend using the demand coefficient of variation (COV) to assess products' forecastability.

Coefficient of variation

The coefficient of variation of a time series is computed as the ratio between its standard deviation and its mean:

$$COV = \sigma/\mu$$

It is often expressed as a percentage.

Unfortunately, as I will show you, historical demand deviation doesn't always correlate with demand forecastability. In many cases, COV will be irrelevant or even misleading for demand planners. As you will see, COV doesn't measure how much *unexpected* variation there is in a time series. It simply measures its variation around the historical mean. In short, measuring COV won't tell you if your product is easily forecastable. COV can be easily inflated if your product is highly seasonal, and even if it's highly forecastable.

10.2.1 COV and simple demand patterns

If you are lucky enough to deal with flat-demand products without any kind of trend, seasonality, or recognizable pattern, COV is a relatively good indicator of overall forecastability (figure 10.5).

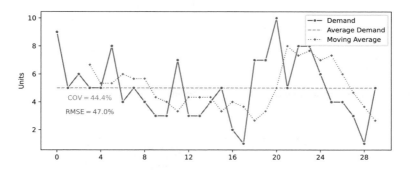

Figure 10.5   **COV vs. moving average (forecasting benchmark) for a stable product**

But, as COV compares historical demand vs. historical demand average, it benefits from *data leakage*. For example, comparing 2020 demand with the 2020 demand average will be much more accurate than comparing 2020 demand with the 2019 demand average. Forecasting is about predicting future demand *without* having access to it.

> **Data leakage**
>
> In the case of forecasting models, a data leakage describes a situation where a model is given pieces of information about the future.

We see this effect in figure 10.5, where COV benefits from data leakage and provides a better result than a simple moving average.

10.2.2 COV and realistic demand patterns

If you work with actual supply chains, you will likely face products following trends and seasonal patterns. In such cases, COV won't give a good indication of forecastability.[29] Look at the two examples in figures 10.6 and 10.7; both cases are easy to forecast for a moving average, yet their COV is high.

---

[29] Some practitioners advise deseasonalizing and removing the trend of demand patterns before computing COV. Unfortunately, these techniques aren't aligned with forecasting practices. When deseasonalizing data, you remove seasonality after the fact, resulting in data leakage (same with untrending). Moreover, deseasonalization and removing trends aren't straightforward techniques and henceforth can't be considered as simple benchmarks.

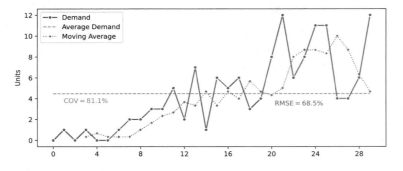

Figure 10.6   COV vs. moving average for a product with trend

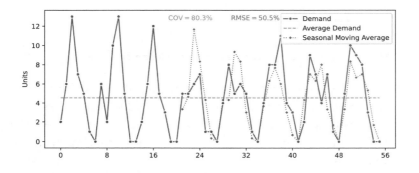

Figure 10.7   COV vs. seasonal moving average for a seasonal product

In conclusion, do not use COV as a proxy for forecastability because it will flag products with trend or seasonality as difficult to forecast. Moreover, COV is benefiting from data leakage. Instead, you should assess products' forecastability by tracking the forecast errors of benchmarks (as discussed earlier in this chapter).

Summary

- Assess your current forecasting accuracy by comparing it against a benchmark. Building upon this technique, we will see in chapter 12 how we can use benchmarks to assess the quality of an entire forecasting process.
- Simple forecasting models (such as moving averages) are straightforward, free, and fair benchmarks.
- Naïve forecasts make poor benchmarks because they aren't accurate enough.

- Using COV as a proxy for forecastability is not a good practice. COV benefits from data leakage and won't properly capture trends and seasonality. Before jumping to this critical step, we need to discuss best practices for measuring forecasting accuracy on broad product portfolios (chapter 11).

- On the other hand, we saw that using COV to assess products' variability is a bad practice. This is because COV can't cope with trends and seasonality and benefits from data leakage. Due to this, COV shouldn't be compared with regular forecasting models.

Measuring forecasting accuracy on a product portfolio

Objective	Data	Metrics	Baseline Model	Review Process

In chapters 9 and 10, we discussed multiple forecasting KPIs trying to assess the quality of a *single* product's forecast (or a single time series). In practice, demand planners deal with hundreds, if not thousands, of products. Unfortunately, when computing a global accuracy metric for various products, you compare pears and apples because products are not all equally important (we will see in table 11.1 an example with nails, hammers, and anvils). Many companies understand this and look at accuracy by product categories rather than for all their products globally at once. Their implicit assumption is that looking at forecasting accuracy globally might be mixing up pears and apples, whereas analyzing products by categories will reduce the heterogeneity.

Are we bound to analyze forecast error by product family, or is there a smarter way to deal with broad product mix?

In this chapter, we will discuss value-weighted KPIs, allowing you to compare pears and apples when forecasting—and focus on the products that matter the most.

11.1 Forecasting metrics and product portfolios

Imagine that you are responsible for forecasting three products: nails, hammers, and anvils. As shown in table 11.1, the absolute forecast error is more significant on the nails (500 pieces) than on the hammers (50 pieces) and the anvils (2). This effect is even more important for the squared error.

Table 11.1 Nails Are the Biggest Offender on Total Forecast Error (the Total on the Squared Error Is Computed as RMSE)

Product	Forecast	Demand	Error	Abs Error	Squared Error
Anvil	10	12	-2	2	4
Hammer	150	100	50	50	2,500
Nail	1,000	1,500	-500	500	250,000
Total	**1,160**	**1,612**	**-452**	**552**	**502**
			-28%	**34%**	**31%**

Obviously, not every SKU is created equal: some bring more profits, some are costly, some require constrained resources (e.g., space), some are of strategic importance . . . while others are just not critical. In short, the impact of each SKU on the supply chain is different, and you want to focus your work on those that matter. In other words, a forecast error on a critical product will have more impact on your supply chain than the same forecast error on a low-value product.

Unfortunately, in our nail-hammer-anvil example, computing metrics across our portfolio would implicitly emphasize the nails due to their massive sales volume.

We could also try to compute metrics based on percentages. But this would result in two other issues. First, every product would be considered equally important. Second, if the demand for a product during one period is 0, it would result in an infinite percentage. In short, averaging percentages across different products and periods is (nearly) always a bad idea. See an example in table 11.2, where the bias is zero when computed based on an average of error percentages. Note that, by chance, in this example, the absolute error total percentage, or MAE%, (the third column starting from the right end) is nearly equivalent to MAPE (last column).

Table 11.2   Percentage Metrics

Product	Demand	Forecast	Error	Absolute Error	Error Percentage	Absolute Percentage Error
Anvil	12	10	−2	2	−16.7%	16.7%
Hammer	100	150	50	50	50.0%	50.0%
Nail	1,500	1,000	−500	500	−33.3%	33.3%
Total	**1,612**	**1,160**	**−452**	**552**	**0.0%**	**33.3%**
			−28%	**34%**		

Remember our main objective: we want our forecasts to be helpful for our supply chain. Therefore, we need to emphasize products that have a more significant impact on our supply chain. In our example, we want a forecast error of 1 anvil to have more importance than a forecast error of 1 nail. To do so, we will have to use value-weighted KPIs, as introduced in the next section.

11.2 *Value-weighted KPIs*

We want to emphasize important products in our forecasting metrics. Let's assume, for the sake of the discussion, that unit costs are a good proxy for products' impact on the supply chain.[30] In this case, we can weight products' forecast errors based on the products' unit costs. I call such weighted metric "*value-weighted* forecast errors" because we allocate more importance to costlier items.

We compute weighted forecast errors (e_w) as $e_w = w(f - d)$, where w is the weight (importance) of a particular product. We can then compute the usual forecasting metrics, as shown in table 11.3.

---

[30] Different businesses might assess product importance based on different criteria. For example, if the business goal is to maximize profits, you can weight forecast errors based on their cash. If it is more important to minimize capital invested, you can weight products by cost.

Table 11.3 Weighted Forecasting KPIs (d_w Is the Weighted Demand)

KPI	Absolute	Percentage
Error	$e_w = w(f - d)$	
Bias	$\frac{1}{n}\sum e_w$	$\dfrac{\sum e_w}{\sum d_w}$
MAE	$\frac{1}{n}\sum |e_w|$	$\dfrac{\sum |e_w|}{\sum |d_w|}$
RMSE	$\sqrt{\frac{1}{n}\sum e_w^2}$	$\dfrac{\sqrt{\frac{1}{n}\sum e_w^2}}{\sum d_w}$

As we weight errors based on costs (€, \$, and so on), we can express forecast errors as value. For example, an absolute forecast error of 5 units on a product worth \$2 is translated into a value-weighted error of \$10.

Let's continue with our nail-hammer-anvil example from the previous chapter, using these new weighted KPIs. As shown in table 11.4, the product that should get your attention is the hammer, with a weighted absolute error of 1000€ (compared to the nails' weighted absolute error of 50€).

Table 11.4 The Hammers Are the Biggest Offenders Now.

Product	Demand	Forecast	Unit cost	Weighted demand	Weighted Forecast	Error	Absolute Error	Squared Error	Weighted Error	Weighted Absolute Error	Weighted Squared Error
Anvil	12	10	50€	600€	500€	–2	2	4	–100€	100€	10,000€
Hammer	100	150	20€	2,000€	3,000€	50	50	2,500	1,000€	1,000€	1,000,000€
Nail	1,500	1,000	0.1€	150€	100€	–500	500	250,000	–50€	50€	2,500€
Total	**1,612**	**1,160**		**2,750€**	**3,600€**	**–452**	**552**	**290**	**850€**	**1,150€**	**581€**
						–28%	**34%**	**18%**	**31%**	**42%**	**21%**

Note that you can weight products based on their costs, margins, or sale prices. Or even based on arbitrary weights to reflect their strategic importance.

As you can see in tables 11.3 and 11.4, RMSE scales poorly to product portfolios. And its value-weighted counterpart doesn't scale well either. As RMSE is squaring errors, it will always put too much emphasis on high-volume items. RMSE might be a good KPI to assess the accuracy of a single product, but it shouldn't be used over portfolios.

Pro Tip: Penalties for over- and under-forecasting?

There is a temptation to penalize (or weight) positive and negative forecast errors differently with a tool such as weighted errors. Obviously, in supply chains, the cost of having one product too many (extra holding costs or spoilage) or one product too few (unhappy clients, lost revenues) is not the same. Nevertheless, you will get biased forecasts by giving more importance to over or under forecasts. This will, in turn, gradually reduce the confidence in the overall forecasting process, until other teams and planners start creating their own projections because they do not trust the main demand forecast anymore. It is always better to balance company priorities regarding risks, costs, and service levels by setting proper service level targets and allocating the right amount of safety stock for each product. For more information, see my book *Inventory Optimizations: Models and Simulations*.

Summary

- You can improve your forecasting KPIs by tracking a cost-weighted version of MAE and bias.
- By using value-weighted KPIs, you are making sure that you focus your attention on the most valuable products. Rather than just on the products with the highest volume. This trick will be critical as we discuss the next steps towards demand forecasting excellence in chapters 12 and 13.

Part 3

Data-driven forecasting process

In part 2, we discussed multiple metrics to assess the inherent quality of a forecast (chapters 8 and 9), used benchmarks to assess the added value of our forecasts (chapter 10), and value-weighted metrics to assess product portfolios (chapter 11). In this third part, we will see how data-driven management will help you achieve demand-planning excellence. In chapter 12, we will discuss the forecast value added framework that will allow you to track the added value of your whole forecasting process (leveraging the benchmarks and value-weighted metrics we discussed in part 2). In chapter 13, using segmentation techniques (such as ABC XYZ), we will see how we can focus the work of demand planners.

Forecast value added

Objective　Data　Metrics　Baseline Model　Review Process

This chapter will show you how to improve your forecasting accuracy (efficacy) and reduce your teams' workload (improving efficiency) using the *Forecast Value Added Framework*. Two birds, one stone.

As we will discuss in the conclusion, Forecast Value Added (FVA) doesn't require massive investment. Its ROI will likely outshine any other demand planning improvement projects. Implementing it should be a priority and the cornerstone of your demand planning improvement journey.

To present this framework, let's imagine the following scenario: you are managing the demand forecasting process of your supply chain. The supply chain is global, with products sold and distributed globally. The first step of your demand planning process is to use forecasting software to create a *baseline forecast.*[31] Then multiple teams provide inputs: first your demand planning team, then salespeople, and finally, the process concludes with a consensus meeting, where the final forecast number is agreed upon (figure 12.1). Unfortunately, as we will see in chapter 16, this final consensus meeting can be more about promoting personal agendas and influence than about forecast future demand in an unbiased way.

Figure 12.1   Your demand forecasting process

Your team achieves a forecast error of 45% and a bias of +4% (as shown in table 12.1). However, you have no idea if you could do better, or if your forecasting software is doing a good job. You're also worried that the consensus meeting might be more about politics and budget adherence than demand forecasting. Moreover, you suspect that your sales team is over forecasting on purpose to avoid shortages.

Table 12.1   Forecasting KPIs

Step	MAE	Bias
Overall Process	45%	+4%

Looking at such a process, the following questions should be addressed:

- Is the forecasting model adequately set up?
- Is the sales team (or any other team) creating bias?
- What assumptions or insights are the teams using when updating the forecast? (We will discuss this in chapter 16.)
- Does the consensus exercise increase or decrease the final accuracy?

Note that for the sake of simplicity, we won't discuss much in this chapter about forecasting lags (chapter 6) or value-weighted metrics (chapter 11). Nevertheless, you should track FVA for all relevant forecasting horizons and use value-weighted metrics. For example, your team might focus too much on

---

[31] I use the term "baseline forecast" to denote the forecast generated by your forecasting software or model. Some call this "statistical forecast", but I prefer a more general term because it could be generated by a machine-learning model.

forecasting lag 1 and overlook subsequent lags. Or you might be reporting a single MAE and Bias value for different products based on their sales volume, despite the fact that their unit value is different (as discussed in chapter 11, this is not a best practice).

12.1　*Comparing your process to a benchmark*

Before jumping into how to track forecast value added across your demand planning process, let's discuss how we can use benchmarks to assess its overall quality.

When discussing forecasting in workshops, I usually get the following question from my clients: *is our current forecasting accuracy good enough?*

As discussed in chapter 10, you can answer this question using forecast benchmarks. Benchmarks can be either *internal* (based on your own data) or *external* (based on industry standards or other outside sources). Let's discuss both approaches in the following sections.

12.1.1　*Internal benchmarks*

The idea of internal benchmarking is simple (figure 12.2):

- Run a simple forecasting algorithm—such as a (seasonal) moving average—through historical periods and track its accuracy.
- Compare the benchmark's results against your model/process. (Do not forget to do this for all relevant lags.)

Figure 12.2　We compare our forecasting process against a benchmark

Using benchmarks to compare yourself with is the best practice to know if you are doing a good job at demand forecasting. The idea is to compare your forecasting process against a benchmark to see by how much extra accuracy you can beat it. This comparison will tell you a lot about process efficiency and efficacy: how much investment (in software and time) do you need to beat a simplistic method? By how much could you beat the benchmark?

To continue with our earlier example, you want to know if your achieved forecast error of 45% and bias of 4% is good or bad. As you can see in table 12.2, your team is beating the benchmark. That's good news.

Table 12.2   Forecasting Process vs. Benchmark

Step	MAE	Bias
Benchmark	52%	–1%
Overall Process	45%	4%

12.1.2 *Industry (external) benchmarks*

Unfortunately, practitioners (and some thought-leaders) often rely on another technique to assess their forecasting accuracy. They compare themselves against industry (external) benchmarks. Indeed, many supply chains want to compare themselves to their competitors and are on the lookout to buy industry benchmarks. Multiple companies (software vendors, consultancy companies, and data providers) would be glad to support you in this endeavor by selling you these benchmarks. They would recommend comparing your supply chain against other companies to gauge your demand planning process.

I do not support this approach, because it compares pears and apples.[32] Here's why:

- Many companies providing benchmarks won't compute forecast accuracy themselves. Instead, they will simply ask companies to respond to a survey. Who knows how your competitors measure forecast accuracy?
- Different companies will compute forecasting accuracy at different aggregation levels (for example, by country, whereas you track it per region) and horizons.
- Different businesses often follow different strategies, resulting in different product portfolio sizes, sales channels, and promotion strategies.[33] These differences will result in *natural* differences in forecasting accuracy between companies within the same industry. For example, you might have 500 products in your catalog, whereas your main low-cost competitor only offers 20. Naturally, this will result in better accuracy. Nevertheless, the fact that your low-cost competitor achieves a good forecast accuracy doesn't say anything about your own demand forecasting process.
- The same holds true for the distribution footprint. You might be present in some markets or channels, whereas your competitors will use a different distribution system.

---

[32] For more information about external benchmarks, see the article "Can We Obtain Valid Benchmarks from Published Surveys of Forecast Accuracy?" By Stephan Kolassa. Foresight (2008). Kolassa (2008).

[33] See the book *Supply Chain Strategy and Financial Metrics* by Bram Desmet. Kogan Page (2018). Desmet (2018).

- Moreover, industry benchmarks are often only available for a specific forecasting horizon (lag). You want to make sure your forecasting process is adding value along the whole relevant horizon (Chapter 6). Not just for a single lag.

In short, industry benchmarks are expensive (and not always available), unreliable (because you do not know how forecasting accuracy is computed), and do not compare apples to apples. Do not use them. Instead, you should always assess the quality of your forecasts by comparing them against internal benchmarks such as a moving average (as discussed in chapter 10).

12.2 *Tracking Forecast Value Added*

As recapped in the previous section (and explained in detail in chapter 10), you learned how to compare your forecasting process to a benchmark to assess its overall added value (*Do we beat a simple benchmark?*). But demand planning is a resource-intensive, multi-step process raising two fundamental questions:

- Does every stage in this process improve the overall accuracy?
- Is the extra accuracy worth the burden?

As various actors input many numbers to come up with the final version, it is difficult to know who adds value and who does not. The ownership and accountability for the forecast are likely to get diluted during the process.

As the demand forecasting process owner, you need to ensure two things:

- *Efficacy:* You want your demand planning team to improve the forecast baseline. Each manual adjustment of the forecast should make it more accurate.

- *Efficiency:* You do not want your team to spend *too much* time working on the forecast. There is a point of diminishing returns. At some point, the time needed to improve your predictions further will not be worth the business value of the extra forecasting accuracy. Basically, there is no point in discussing if you should change a product's forecast by 0.1% for two days.

To track these two (efficacy: *Are we improving the forecast?* and efficiency: *Are we making good use of our time?*), we will use the Forecast Value Added framework (FVA) as introduced in the next Section.

12.2.1 *Process efficacy*

The idea of the Forecast Value Added framework (FVA)[34] is to track the accuracy of each step in a forecasting process (model, planners, sales team, consensus).[35] As shown in table 12.3 and figure 12.3, each team is given an FVA score based on the added accuracy they achieved, compared to the previous step.

Table 12.3   Forecast Value Added Dashboard

Step	MAE	FVA	Bias	FVA
Benchmark	52%		–1%	
Forecasting Model	45%	+7	–3%	–2
Demand Planners	43%	+2	1%	+2
Sales team	45%	–2	5%	–4
Consensus	45%	+0	4%	+1

Tracking the added value of each team will promote ownership and accountability—both are key process excellence. Indeed, performing an FVA analysis of the whole forecasting process (demand planners, salespeople, senior management)[36] will ensure that each team owns their predictions and is accountable for the achieved accuracy. The quality of anyone's forecast edition won't be diluted in the overall accuracy achieved. Moreover, as you track each step's added value, you will have the right analytics to reduce most judgmental biases (more about these in chapter 16).

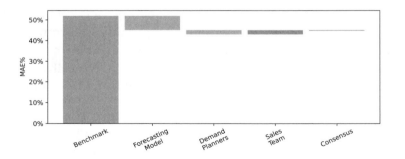

Figure 12.3   Waterfall visualization of MAE throughout the process (tracking bias using a waterfall is trickier because it can be both positive and negative).

---

[34] The FVA framework was introduced in Is forecasting a waste of time? by Michael Gilliland. *Supply Chain Management Review.* 2002.
[35] You should also track customer forecasts: they are too often trusted but do not always add any value. Moreover, identifying errors is a great opportunity for customer engagement and alignment.
[36] You can even track the FVA of each individual separately.

Let's continue with our example (see the FVA metrics in table 12.4) and look at what demand planners, salespeople, and the management team were thinking when editing the forecast. As you can see in figure 12.4, some teams (here, the salespeople and the consensus meeting) are biased and want to achieve specific goals when reviewing the forecast. We will discuss these intentional biases further in chapter 16.

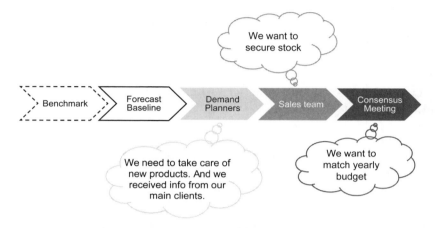

Figure 12.4   Thought-process when editing the forecast

12.2.2 *Process efficiency*

Forecast value add is meant to ensure that each team member adds value compared to the previous one (*efficacy*). *And* that team members don't spend too much time editing the forecast (*efficiency*). To measure efficiency, we have to track roughly the time spent on each step in the forecasting process.

Table 12.4   Tracking Working Time with FVA

Step	Person-hours	MAE	FVA	Bias	FVA
Benchmark		52%		−1%	
Forecasting Model		45%	+7	−3%	−2
Demand Planners	72	43%	+2	1%	+2
Sales team	20	45%	−2	5%	−4
Consensus	8	45%	+0	4%	+1

With the help of FVA, you will quickly realize that the marginal improvement of each new team working on the forecast is decreasing. It might be easy to improve the most significant shortcomings of a forecasting model (like product introductions). However, it is much more challenging to improve a forecast that has already been reviewed by various professional teams relying on multiple sources of information.

Past a certain point, working more on the forecast will not be worth it. By tracking both the time spent, and the added value, FVA will help you allocate just the right amount of resources to your process.

12.2.3 *Best practices*

Let's review a few extra best practices when using the Forecast Value Added framework.

- The objective of FVA is to help management bring the best out of their teams. Don't overreact to a few negative FVA rounds by ditching parts of the forecast process. The point is to find the root causes of the under-performance and fix the process (most likely by removing biases, promoting ownership, and aligning incentives—more about this in chapter 16). Removing steps of the process that should, in theory, add value should be the last resort.
- Do not hesitate to track and report FVA by product group, channel, or region. Especially if different sales channels (or business units) utilize different information, teams, and buying behaviors.
- You should track FVA over the whole relevant forecasting horizon (chapter 6).
- You should also use FVA together with value-weighted KPIs (chapter 11) to focus on the most critical items.

More tips and best practices can be found in the conclusions drawn by Fildes and Goodwin in their 2007 article "Good and Bad Judgment in Forecasting: Lessons from Four Companies" (Foresight), where they investigated the demand planning process of four British companies.[37] Here are their main findings:

- *Do not spend time on minor adjustments:* They are most likely within the error margin. They saw that planners were making numerous minor adjustments to the forecasts, bringing nearly no added value and consuming time. (The need to act is a common cognitive bias.)

---

[37] Fildes, et al., 2007.

- *Focus on significant adjustments:* They are more likely to improve accuracy as senior management requires more explanations. Moreover, larger adjustments carry higher (personal) risks if they are wrong.
- *Track the number of positive and negative adjustments:* Planners tend to be overly optimistic in their adjustments, resulting in over forecasting. This tendency for positive adjustments can be explained easily: it takes more courage and data to bring bad news than good news. It is also a more pleasurable experience to share good news and perspectives with your colleagues than to be the one reducing the expected sales. As Fildes and Goodwin noted that most positive adjustments decreased the accuracy (while most negative adjustments positively impacted accuracy), they provocatively suggested banning positive adjustments altogether. Their solution might be a bit extreme, but if you face too many positive adjustments you can start tracking FVA separately for positive and negative adjustments. This should be an eye-opener for biased teams. More about the reasons behind these biases in chapter 16.

Words of advice from Michael Gilliland

Michael Gilliland introduced the forecast value added framework in 2002 in his article "Is forecasting a waste of time?" (*Supply Chain Management Review*). In 2010, he published his book focusing on avoiding bad practices for demand planning: *The Business Forecasting Deal* (Wiley, 2010).[38] As explained there (pp. 97-98):

"Since naive forecasts can be surprisingly difficult to beat, the results of FVA analysis may be rather embarrassing to those participants who are failing to add value. Therefore, present the results tactfully. Your objective is to improve the forecasting process—not necessarily to humiliate anyone. You may also want to present initial results privately, to avoid public embarrassment for the non-value adders."

As a consultant doing FVA analysis for a client, it is great news if their forecasting quality is worse than a simple benchmark. You can easily help the client improve their forecasts by stopping whatever they are doing and using the benchmark instead. A thorough FVA analysis will help you identify the process steps and participants ruining accuracy.

SETTING OBJECTIVES

Once you have a proper set of accuracy metrics, it is tempting for management to set firm targets to demand planners. However, as management promises bonuses and incentives if planners meet these targets, they also incentivize planners to find a way to hack the metrics. For example, planners could only

---

[38] Gilliland, 2002 and 2010.

track accuracy at a specific lag or at a high (irrelevant?) forecasting aggregation level. Creative team members could even develop accommodating specific rules to compute forecasting accuracy.[39]

When setting accuracy targets (or KPIs in general), pay attention to the following words of warning:

- *Do not set arbitrary targets*: Instead, investigate what is reasonably achievable (in the case of forecasting accuracy, you should use forecasting benchmarks). Always keep in mind that external factors also drive performance. By definition, team members have no impact on external factors and can't be blamed (or rewarded) for their effects. For example, you cannot expect the same accuracy in 2020 as in 2019 (Covid).

- Do not use targets to "reward and punish." Indeed, as you put too much pressure (or rewards) on specific targets (or KPIs), there is a high temptation for your team to hack the metric (often to the detriment of real business value). Instead, use metrics to "discuss and improve": discuss how your team members can improve on some metrics without harming overall business values and by collaborating with their business partners. Always remember that despite your team's best efforts, a specific KPI can deteriorate over time due to external conditions. They shouldn't be blamed for that.

12.2.4 *How do you get started?*

FVA is simple to understand and will be the backbone of your demand forecasting improvement journey. But it requires a lot of data because you need to track numerous forecast versions: one per team working on the forecast and one per lag. Moreover, you'll need to invest in automation to run it smoothly: you can't spend days creating a monthly dashboard. For example, imagine you want to forecast demand six months ahead and have three teams (planners, sales, management) working on your forecast (plus your baseline forecast and a benchmark). You'll need to use 30 different forecasts versions (5 steps x 6 lags) to compute FVA for each lag for each step.

I then advise two ways to get started:

- You can easily compare your consensus forecast against a benchmark: Run a moving average of your past sales and compare it with your forecast. Good demand planning processes should beat fine-tuned benchmarks.

---

[39] For example, I have seen multiple companies not tracking forecast errors when demand was zero. I have also witnessed a consultancy company presenting forecast accuracy results to a management committee. Their results included a small footnote reading, « results exclude the 5% top offenders. »

The extent of the improvement over the benchmark depends on your supply chain's underlying demand patterns. For example, if your demand is highly promotion-driven, it is likely that you can beat a benchmark by 20% (as benchmarks do not include any information about promotions). In any case, if you can't beat a benchmark by more than 5%, it is likely that you have room for improvement.

- To run FVA at scale, you'll need specialized software or to create your own automated data pipeline. Unfortunately, many forecasting software do not offer these possibilities.[40] And creating this data pipeline yourself is technically possible with Python or any other programming language, but not straightforward.

Having covered process efficacy and efficiency and having looked at the best practices, we're in a good place to wrap up and look to the next steps.

Summary

- The Forecast Value Added framework will help you to ensure that each team makes meaningful changes by making every team the owner of their adjustments.

- Combine FVA with value-weighted KPIs will ensure that your teams will focus on the most valuable products.

- By looking at the bias and accuracy obtained by each team will allow you to spot bad practices and problems. In chapter 16, you will learn how to deal with intentional biases (read politics) and unintentional biases (read cognitive biases).

- Do not compare your forecasting accuracy against industry benchmarks. These benchmarks are irrelevant because they aren't using the same scope of products and markets, are expensive, and are not consistently tracked using appropriate metrics. Instead, use forecasting benchmarks as explained in chapter 10.

---

[40] To assess your FVA, you can try SKU Science (https://skuscience.com), the forecasting platform I cofounded. It offers a free trial allowing you to load your consensus forecast and compare its baseline forecast.

What do you review? ABC XYZ segmentations and other methods

Objective · Data · Metrics · Baseline Model · Review Process

I want to review my demand forecast. Which product should I check first?

Forecasting models usually consider each forecast-item independently. Computing power is virtually unlimited, so you want your model to create the best possible forecast for every single product. On the other end, demand planners do not have the time to inspect every single product (in every single location, for every client). As a demand planner, you need to scale up from analyzing in detail one single item to working on a portfolio with thousands of SKUs. During each forecast exercise, you have the opportunity to review a limited selection of your products. On which items should you spend your time?

In chapter 11, you learned to use value-weighted KPIs to highlight the most important products in a portfolio. In chapter 12, you learned to use the *Forecast Value Added* framework to ensure that anyone working on the forecast adds value. But these two frameworks will not tell you which products you should focus your attention on when reviewing forecasts. This is the focus of this chapter.

You have to prioritize your work by focusing on the most important products for your supply chain, and for which you are the most likely to add accuracy compared to the initial *baseline forecast*. This chapter will discuss a new framework—ABC XYZ classification—that will help you identify products matching these two conditions. We will also discuss more advanced ideas for even better focus.

13.1 ABC XYZ segmentations

Before jumping into the discussion on how ABC analysis should be used and set up, let's take the time to define ABC XYZ categorizations.

13.1.1 ABC analysis

If 20% of my products represent 80% of my sales, I'd better start by reviewing these.

ABC analysis is a simplistic, arbitrary technique to categorize items based on two thresholds along one dimension. Items are segregated into three categories (A, B, and C). Group A contains the *critical few*, whereas the *trivial many* are categorized as C.[41]

Supply chain practitioners usually use ABC analyses to categorize products based on volume or profits (as shown in table 13.1):

Table 13.1   **ABC segmentation based on volume**

	A Class	B Class	C Class
% of items	5%	15%	80%
% of volume	20-60%	20-50%	5-20%
Priority	High	Mid	Low

- The top 5% of products are classified as A, and they usually account for 40% of the total volume. These are the few critical items (also called A movers).
- The following top 15% are classified as B. They usually account for another 40% of the total volume.
- Finally, the bottom 80% of products are classified as C, and they usually only account for 20% of the total volume. These are the trivial many.

This categorization implicitly assumes that a few percent of a supply chain's products (*A Class products*) are driving most of the revenues (or profits) and that you should focus your attention on these.

---

[41] This concept is also called the Pareto analysis or the 80/20 rule (because 20% of the causes drive 80% of the consequences).

As shown in table 13.2, you can also set up your ABC classification by defining classes as groups of products accounting for x% of your total (historical) sales. For example, you would define A Class Products as "Products contributing to 60% of my total sales" rather than "Top 5% of products".

Table 13.2 ABC with Thresholds Based on % of Total Volume

	A Class	B Class	C Class
% of items	5-15%	15-30%	50-80%
% of volume	60%	20%	20%
Priority	High	Mid	Low

13.1.2 *ABC XYZ analysis*

An ABC XYZ analysis is a two-dimensional segmentation along the ABC and XYZ axis. Because there are two dimensions, items will be assigned to nine categories.

As shown in figure 13.1, you can, for example, classify items based on their total contribution to volume (ABC axis, in units) and profits (XYZ axis, in value). By doing so, you will obtain a classification ranging from high-volume, high-profit products to low-volume, low-profit products.

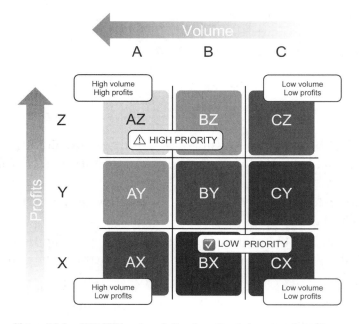

Figure 13.1   ABC XYZ segmentation based on volumes and profits

13.2 *Using ABC XYZ for demand forecasting*

Planners often use ABC XYZ classifications to identify the most important products within their portfolios. But, if not correctly set up, these matrices will not point to the relevant products and lure you away from efficiently reviewing your forecasts. Moreover, as with any simplification tool, ABC XYZ suffers limitations, even when it is adequately set up. Don't trust it blindly.

Let's review the best (and the bad) practices when using this framework.

Our objective is to help demand planners to review their forecasts by pointing them to the *most critical products* where they are the *most likely to add value* (on top of the baseline forecast). To support this review process, we set up our ABC XYZ matrix with one dimension denoting products' importance and the other one their forecastability. We will assume for now that we are most likely to add value to low-forecastability products (figure 13.2). See chapter 10 for a discussion on forecasting errors, benchmarks, demand variability, and forecastability.

In short, we assume that low-forecastability, high-importance products should be reviewed first. Whereas high-forecastability, low-importance products can be left to your forecasting engine.

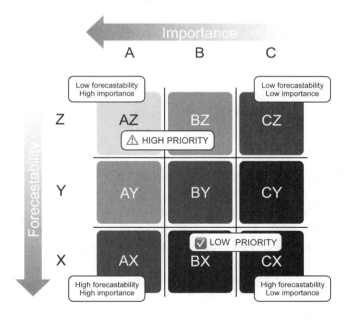

Figure 13.2   ABC XYZ matrix with products' importance and forecastability

In practice, we need to find a way to categorize products (using quantitative metrics) along two dimensions: importance and forecastability, which we'll cover next.

We could use various criteria to classify products: historical demand, future forecasts, profits, COV, forecast errors, etc. Which ones should we use?

13.2.1 Products' importance

To identify critical products, we need to use a metric that is both *forward-looking* (What are the important products in the next X months?) and *value-weighted* (Let's focus on the most valuable products).

- *Forward-looking:* We want to highlight products that will be important *in the future*, so we should segment products along the ABC axis based on their demand forecasts.
- *Value-weighted:* We will use value-weighted forecasts (chapter 11) to denote products' criticality and ensure that we focus on the future most valuable products.

Bad practice

Many practitioners still rely on segmenting products based on historical sales. This is a bad practice. It is not because you sold a lot of a product over the last three months that it will be your top seller in the following six months. (Think about all the seasonal effects, promotions, and trends.) Moreover, you should always look at unconstrainted demand rather than constrained sales (chapters 2 and 3).

In short, by using forecasts instead of historical demand, you will be forward-looking and on the lookout for what's next.

13.2.2 Products' forecastability

You want to highlight products where your forecast engine is likely to be wrong on the XYZ axis. To do so, you can classify products based on their historical forecast error (computed in relative terms using a combination of MAE% a Bias%, for example). By tracking this metric, you highlight products for which your forecasting engine couldn't deliver satisfactory results on its own.

Bad practice

Some software platforms, consultants, and practitioners still advise using products' demand variability (or coefficient of variation, COV) to differentiate them along the XYZ axis. However, as discussed in chapter 10, this is a poor idea because COV is a poor indicator of forecastability. Indeed, products with trends or seasonality will display high COV. Yet, these can be easily forecastable.

13.2.3 *ABC XYZ limitations*

ABC XYZ classifications represented state-of-the-art analysis half a century ago when demand and supply planners couldn't rely on computers to perform automated, insightful analyses. Instead, they had to analyze products' inventory and forecasts manually. As they lacked time to do thorough investigations, they used simple rules to identify the most important products.

As with any simplification tool, ABC XYZ matrices come with issues, namely:

- *A limited number of dimensions:* By definition, ABC XYZ only considers two aspects to categorize elements. On the other hand, your products—and supply chains in general—are much more complex than a two-dimensional representation. As a result, even our *smart* ABC XYZ classification will miss relevant information such as supply lead times, lead time reliability, shelf-life, risk of obsolescence, business criticality, etc.

- *Arbitrary, limited thresholds:* An ABC XYZ matrix contains only two arbitrary thresholds per dimension. Are the best B products *really* different than the worst A? Not really. This A/B segregation threshold is purely arbitrary. Some analyses require a much more granular level of details.

In short, ABC XYZ is a good tool for performing simple analyses and recommendations. But it suffers limitations. On the other hand, we now have the analytic capabilities to scale complex, smarter logics to a whole dataset.

13.3 *Beyond ABC XYZ: Smart multi-criteria classification*

Let's recap our initial statement: as a planner, your time is limited. You want to focus your reviews on the few products where you will have the most significant impact. So, the question is which items should you review?

By using ABC XYZ segmentation with the best practices discussed earlier, you will spend most of your time working on future best-sellers with the highest historical forecast errors. While letting your forecast engine work on less relevant and more stable products.

Unfortunately, only looking at these future best sellers and products with high historical forecast error will leave many essential products unchecked. Instead, multiple criteria should be used: shelf life, costs, available information, business criticality, among others. Let's discuss a few ideas in detail:

- Focus on products for which you have information that the baseline model is unaware of (such as promotions, marketing, client actions). We will discuss this crucial best practice further in chapter 16.

- Spend time on new products' introduction. These are typically items for which you have more information than your model.

- Review items manifesting strange behaviors such as consistent over/under-forecasting or massive demand shifts since last periods.

- Spend more time on high-cost products (or products with longer lead times) because forecast errors will be more expensive for these products. Critical items could be products with higher holding costs than usual, such as products requiring special storage conditions (frozen products) or with a short shelf-life (food, medicine).

- At the end of a season, seasonal products risk becoming leftovers—ultimately resulting in deadstock. Careful reviews (and actions) are needed.

- Some products can also be strategically critical, even if their sales volumes are relatively low. This can be because you signed specific service-level agreements with your clients. Or because these products are necessary for bigger orders to be made. For example, you will not buy an expensive piece of equipment if you aren't sure that you can also buy the necessary maintenance parts.

- Review together products that are usually sold together. For example, if you sell nuts and bolts and the forecast of one is increased, the forecast of the second should follow.

Reviewing products' forecasts requires using advanced, granular, multi-criteria analyses. Unfortunately, the two-dimensional, arbitrary ABC XYZ classifications will never be entirely up to this challenge. How could you fit so many criteria in two dimensions? On the other hand, modern software offers advanced analytics capabilities (Python is your friend) that you can leverage to highlight products requiring your attention. You can, for example, summarize these criteria using a simple star-based rating system. Five-star products should be reviewed first. One-star products, last. Here are a few ideas on how to allocate these stars:

- *Good overall forecastability:* –1 star
- *Small volume/value:* –1 star
- *End-of-season:* +1 stars
- *Promotions:* +2 stars
- *Brand new product:* +3 stars
- *Critical product:* +3 stars

Attention

It is not because a product is critical that you should increase its forecast to be "on the safe side." Do not confuse a demand forecast and a supply plan (see chapter 2). It is up to the inventory manager to assess the required amount of safety stocks based on products' costs, risks, as well as demand and supply uncertainty. So, if you want to be protected against shortages, it is *not* up to demand planners (or any other team such as salespeople and customer service) to increase forecasts. Biased forecasts will lead to chaos over the long term. They will deteriorate the overall confidence in the forecasting process until other teams start using their own predictions. Or start double guessing amounts: "I know demand planners usually overinflate the forecast, so I will reduce my stock targets to compensate."

Summary

- ABC XYZ is a practical tool to help demand planners focus on important products where they are likely to make an impact.

- These classifications are especially appreciated as they are simple to understand and set up.

- Pay attention to using adequate metrics in your classification: *value-weighted future forecasts* for the ABC axis; and *historical forecast errors* for the XYZ axis. These two metrics will capture both forward-looking importance and historical forecastability.

- Conversely, avoid following bad practices, such as using backward-looking metrics (historical sales) or demand variability (COV) as a proxy for forecastability.

- You can also leverage more advanced analytics by categorizing and prioritizing your products using more criteria such as business-criticality, shelf-life, (holding) costs, supply reliability, promotions, and launches.

Part 4

Forecasting methods

In this last part, we will discuss forecasting methods. We will discuss statistical methods in chapter 14, followed by more advanced machine-learning techniques in chapter 15, where we will compare both approaches regarding complexity and expected results. Finally, we will discuss judgmental forecasts in chapter 16 (when to use them and how to avoid intentional and unintentional biases).

Statistical forecasting

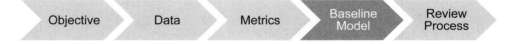

Objective ▸ Data ▸ Metrics ▸ **Baseline Model** ▸ Review Process

Statistical forecasting models can be roughly divided into two types: Time series forecasting, the most common one, and predictive models. This division can be a bit artificial at times—you could use both approaches in a single model—but let's keep it for now because it will simplify our understanding of the topic.

14.1 Time series forecasting

Time series models look at historical demand patterns (trend and seasonality) and extrapolate them into the future. To do so, they usually decompose demand into three subcomponents: level, trend, and seasonality. Most time series forecasting models are also called *univariate* as they only use one variable (historical demand) to predict an outcome (future demand).

> **Definition: Univariate models**
>
> A model is said to be univariate if it only uses a single variable to predict another one. In our case of supply chain demand forecasting, it means that we only use historical demand to predict future demand

14.1.1   *Demand components: Level, trend, and seasonality*

- *Level:* The level is the average value around which the demand varies over time. As you can observe in figure 14.1, the level often looks like a smoothed version of the demand.
  Example: "On average, we sell ten books per day." Figure 14.1 illustrates the sales level of Toyota in Norway between 2007 and 2017.

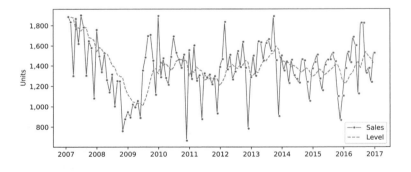

Figure 14.1   Historical sales and level of Toyota cars in Norway[42]

- *Trend:* The trend translates the idea of a consistent change in level from one period to another. It is usually expressed as an additive amount because it is risky to extrapolate *multiplicative* trends (or growth rate) when forecasting demand. If your forecast engine allows multiplicative trends by default, I recommend deactivating it.
  Example: "Sales are growing by 100 extra units each month."

---

[42] The data is compiled by the Opplysningsrådet for Veitrafikken (OFV), a Norwegian organization in the automotive industry. It was initially retrieved by Dmytro Perepølkin and published on Kaggle.

Figure 14.2 illustrates the sales level and trend of BMW in Norway.

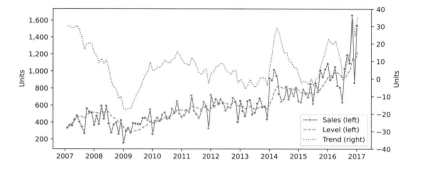

Figure 14.2 Historical sales, level, and trend of BMW car sales in Norway

- *Seasonality:* Seasonal products—with high and low seasons—are common for many supply chains across the globe, as many different factors (such as recurring promotions or holidays) cause seasonality (figure 14.3). Technically, seasonal factors determine how demand is spread through a recurring cycle (such as a day, a week, or a year). Over an entire seasonal cycle, the total seasonal impact should be 0: a high season must be compensated by a low season at another time.

  Example: "We sell 30% more than usual in Q2, 20% less than usual in Q3, and 10% less in Q4."

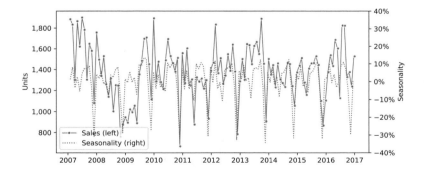

Figure 14.3 Historical sales and seasonality of Toyota in Norway

This level-trend-seasonality decomposition is especially useful for planners. They can read how the model interprets historical demand patterns and projects them in the future.

Time series forecasting is usually done using *exponential smoothing* or ARIMA models. (Exponential smoothing models are also known as *Holt-Winters* based on the two academicians who published the models in the late 1950s.) In practice, both can spot and extrapolate trends and seasonality. Moreover, they can be automatically tuned by an algorithm. See my book *Data Science for Supply Chain Forecasting,* to learn how to implement exponential smoothing in Python and Excel. You can also read *Forecasting: Principles and Practice* by Rob J. Hyndman and George Athanasopoulos, which is freely available online.[43]

> **Pro Tip**
>
> Most software forecasting engines assume that if you have a product with a seasonality, it also follows a trend. This is not always true (as shown in figure 14.3). Using a too-complex model to forecast a simple demand pattern results in a risk of overfitting historical demand patterns and failing to extrapolate meaningful patterns in the future. Furthermore, if little data is available, a simple moving average model will often outperform more complex models (that are likely to overfit fake patterns observed in the short historical period).

14.1.2 Setting up time series models

Time series models are especially practical as you only need historical demand to set them up. This is why most supply chains still rely on these models to forecast their demand: they are easy to understand and set up and do not need much data. Note that, in order to pick up seasonal patterns, a few cycles (three to five) will be needed. For example, three to four years of historical demand will be enough to capture monthly seasonality. Unfortunately, many vendors and consultants still advise using three years of data to generate statistical forecasts. I do not support this practice. Three years might be enough to spot monthly seasonality in some cases. Still, it opens the door to *overfitting*. The model will overreact to historical random variations by assuming patterns such as trends or seasonality. This will result in great historical accuracy (showcasing outstanding accuracy metrics) but poor accuracy on actual future forecasts. It is time we move on from this three-year limitation.

14.2 Predictive analytics and demand drivers

Another way to forecast demand is to look at *demand drivers;* understand how these factors impact demand; then forecast future demand based on these drivers. This is often called *predictive analytics.*

---

[43] It is freely available on https://otexts.com/fpp3/. Hyndman, et al., 2021.

Demand driver

Demand drivers are the factors influencing the purchasing behaviors of businesses and consumers. These drivers can be internal to your company (e.g., prices, marketing budget, or promotions) or external (e.g., weather or competitive activity).

Note that some prefer using the more academic term *explanatory variables* or *exogenous factors* to describe what I call *demand drivers*. For the sake of simplicity, I will stick to using demand drivers, but feel free to use your favorite terminology.

For example, let's imagine you want to forecast ice cream demand for next week Monday. A great idea would be to look at the weather forecast for next week—people tend to buy more ice creams on a hot and sunny day. You would also want to know if the waffle truck (your indirect competition) will be around, if school is out, or if a game will take place (figure 14.4). All these events are demand drivers and knowing them beforehand will allow you to (drastically) improve your future demand forecast.

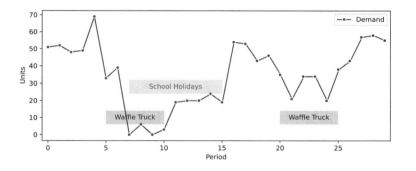

Figure 14.4 Impact of school holidays and competition (waffle truck) on demand for ice cream

Let's take a more detailed look at demand drivers in the following section.

14.2.1 Demand drivers

We can categorize demand drivers into two main categories: *internal* and *external* drivers.

- *Internal drivers:* These are all the elements impacting demand that your company has control over. Demand is usually driven by:
  - Pricing
  - Promotions
  - Marketing

- Events
- Shortages and substitution products[44]
- *External drivers:* These are the drivers external to your company. Companies are often impacted by:
  - Holidays
  - Weather
  - Macroeconomic indicators
  - Competition
  - Online visibility (e.g., number of online searches)
  - Legal and regulatory

You can see in table 14.1 the main demand drivers that you are likely to encounter in supply chains.

Table 14.1   Main Demand Drivers

Driver	History	Future
Promotions	✓	? Planned for medium-term
Events	✓	✓
Marketing	✓	? Usually short-term only
Pricing	✓	? Usually short-term only
Shortages	✓	✓
Weather	✓	? Very short-term
Competition	✗	✗
Macroeconomic indicators	✓	? Works if leading indicators

Let's discuss them one by one while asking ourselves three critical questions:

1. How and to what extent do they impact demand?
2. How easy is it to access historical data?
3. How easy is it to access future data? As we will discuss, accessing demand drivers' future data is essential. For example, you possibly cannot use weather to predict demand six months ahead.

---

[44] Historical shortages are a specific case as companies do not have control over them. But I consider them as internal demand drivers because they are directly related to your own supply chain and operations. See chapter 3 for a discussion about capturing unconstrained demand in case of shortages.

PROMOTIONS

If you have a promotion-driven business, promotions most likely have a massive impact on demand. Because they can be easily tracked and planned, they should be included in your model (figure 14.5).

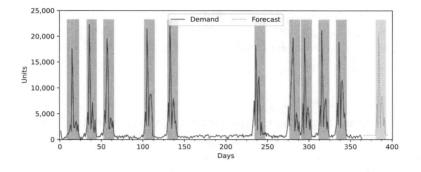

Figure 14.5 **Impact of promotions on demand and forecast (FMCG distributor)**

Difficulties can arise with indirect promotions (such as *"buy one today and get a 10-euro coupon to spend next month"*). Moreover, some businesses also like to run various types of discounts (from *"Buy two, get one."* to *"Happy birthday! You get a discount of 10% on everything."*), which makes data gathering difficult. In such a case, each type of promotion could be modeled individually. Otherwise, you could track actual discounted sales prices rather than if there was a promotion or not (and model the impact of discounts).

Promotions can also be difficult to model as they can result in preorders, clients delaying their purchases in expectation, or rebounds effects (these effects are sometimes called *self-cannibalization*). As figure 14.6 illustrates, when doing recurring (or announced) promotions, you can expect lower demand before and after your main sales periods. (As a personal example, I like to *wait* for Black Friday to buy goods, only to realize that the goods I want are often out-of-stock or not discounted.)

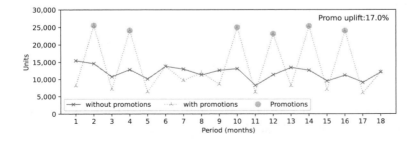

Figure 14.6 **Demand scenarios and self-cannibalization (automotive manufacturer)**

As a last modeling difficulty, most promotions are often only run once or twice a year (think Black Friday or Valentine's Day). Learning demand patterns based on a couple of observations only is challenging for any model. This can even get more complicated if you deal with short-life-cycle products (typically anything related to technology or fashion).

Finally, on the business side, promotions can be run on short-term notice (for example, to get rid of excess inventory). Obviously, promotions that aren't included in time in the forecast won't be correctly forecasted—even by the most advanced forecasting model.

Pro tip: Data cleaning, promotions uplifts, and demand baseline

Some planners like cleaning out historical promotions before forecasting future demand. It is not a good practice to manually clean history because this is inefficient and an open door for *data hacking* (modifying historical demand will allow your planners to raise their accuracy artificially). If you are regularly cleaning historical promotions, consider investing in a forecasting tool where you can flag promotions so that the tool can automate this cleaning for you. A better solution would be to choose a forecasting engine that can forecast promotions directly so you will be able to analyze the expected sales uplift.

EVENTS

When it comes to demand forecasting, events are (very) similar to promotions—both in terms of how they impact and how to collect historical data and plan future occurrences. Moreover, events usually come along with promotions or discounts. Finally, events are straightforward to track as they are often planned months in advance.

MARKETING

Marketing budgets (including online advertisement) also impact demand and the number of clients. Unfortunately, collecting these budgets and linking them to the sales of specific products can be more tedious than with promotions.

PRICING

Price should impact demand—if not, it is time you raise your prices. Unfortunately, including prices in a demand forecasting model is difficult for a few reasons:

- *Inconsistent prices:* In B2B, clients might enjoy different prices or quarterly/yearly discounts. In such a case, you might have to forecast demand per article, channel, and customer group to fully grasps the impact of pricing and discounts.

- *Lack of variation:* Many brick-and-mortar B2C retailers rarely change their prices so as not to confuse or frustrate their clients. Think about your local bakery: they won't change the price of bread every day to find the best-selling price. On the other hand, e-retailers (such as Amazon) have become masters at experimenting with pricing.[45]

- *No long-term view:* Most supply chains do not have a clear vision of their future prices. Planning prices is especially challenging when you need to plan the price of every product for the next 18 months in every market and channel—especially if inflation is lurking around the corner. Just as with promotions, you could enjoy a fantastic model properly capturing the impact of pricing on demand; but not be able to leverage it to forecast future demand as you can't plan your prices months in advance. In such a case, you can still use your model to generate different price scenarios.

- *Sensitive subject:* Discussing pricing can be challenging as it is critical to a company's income and marketing positioning. Moreover, pricing often involves multiple stakeholders, and future prices might be confidential.

On the other hand, companies that have to signal massive price raises (often due to increased prices of raw materials) know that such announcements impact demand (as shown in figure 14.7). These announcements—rather than the detailed prices—could also be included in a forecasting engine.

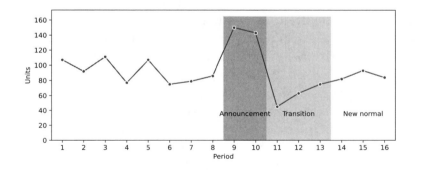

Figure 14.7   Impact of price raise (announcement then transition) on demand

SHORTAGES

Shortages censor unconstrained demand as they limit your ability to collect orders (chapter 3). As you can see in figure 14.8, a model that doesn't leverage shortage information will struggle to provide any relevant forecast. Worst,

---

[45] As I could personally witness with my two previous books.

these forecasts will get stuck in the *sales forecasting vicious circle* we discussed in chapter 2; shortages tend to reinforce themselves as sales forecasts go to zero. On the other hand, if your model understands that some periods suffered shortages, it will be able to censor these zero-sales periods and stick to an unconstrained demand forecast. Remember, we should forecast *unconstrained* demand (assuming no shortages): how many goods do your clients want? If you need to populate a sales or revenue forecast, you can constrain this demand forecast *later* by including current and expected shortages in it (chapter 2).

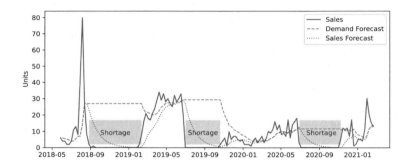

Figure 14.8   Impact of shortages on demand (online retailer)

Shortages are easy to track and critical to understanding demand patterns. It should be a priority for your model to take them into account. Nevertheless, it can become challenging if you deal with monthly forecasting. Indeed, you can be out of stock for a few days during a month. In such a case, the impact on demand is unclear: *Will your clients wait for a few days? Did they go to the competition, or will they buy more after to compensate?*

Tracking shortages can also be challenging for retailers. First, inventory levels are not always correctly recorded. Moreover, in some cases, the only pieces left in stock could be in the storage room rather than on the shelves (resulting in lost sales despite having inventory). If you face these situations, you might have to develop a model to detect shortages based on zero-sales periods. If you spot zero sales for a few consecutive periods on a product, you might flag this period as a shortage (even if the inventory level is positive).

HOLIDAYS

Regarding data collection, holidays are usually one of the most straightforward demand drivers to deal with: they are typically fixed and known in advance.[46]

---

[46] If you use Python, the library *holidays* is your friend. It contains bank holidays for countless countries. You can access it here: https://pypi.org/project/holidays/.

On the contrary, some specific holidays or celebrations, such as French school holidays or Ramadan, take place on different dates each year, which makes forecasting more complicated—especially as these holidays can spread partially across two months (making monthly forecasting especially difficult).

WEATHER

The weather profoundly impacts end-customer habits and many products' consumption rates. You might wait for the rain to stop to do the groceries; you might eat more ice cream as the weather becomes warmer. Short-term forecasts for retailers might benefit from using such data (including both the temperature and the overall weather condition). But, unfortunately, we can't predict the weather accurately more than two weeks ahead. So, using weather data might only be relevant for very short-term forecasts.

MACROECONOMIC INDICATORS

The overall economy is also impacting supply chains across the globe. Think global shortages, inflation, wars, tariffs, Covid, unemployment rates, economic growth, raw material prices, energy prices . . . . Each of these will impact your demand (and supply!) in various ways. For example, many companies face the impact of raw material prices and want to forecast them to predict future costs, revenues, and demand.

Unfortunately, you usually do not know raw material prices, unemployment rate, or inflation in advance. You can nevertheless do scenario forecasting, or you can try to forecast the indicators themselves before including them in your model, but that's usually not a robust (and accurate) technique.

FORECASTING WITH LEADING INDICATORS

A better idea is to use *leading indicators*. These are macro-economic indicators that impact demand with a certain delay (as illustrated in figure 14.9). So, as you know a leading indicator current state, you have an edge to forecast future demand. For example, the current number of processed building permits drives future demand for construction projects (and all the underlying products and household appliances). We can also see a business' order book as a leading indicator of its future commercial success. So, if your business collects preorders, you can reach outstanding forecasting accuracy (over a short-term horizon) by using your order book as a demand driver.

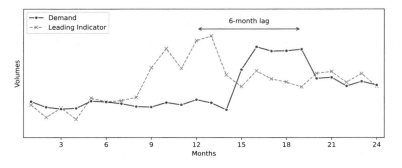

Figure 14.9   Demand and its leading indicator (six-month lag)

We've just covered multiple drivers, but before you implement them into your forecasting process (or model), you should first consider the complexities and challenges they may introduce. We'll consider these challenges next.

14.2.2 Challenges

Including various demand drivers in a forecasting engine is often a promising idea—attracting senior leadership attention. But it comes with challenges. Let's review the main ones:

- *Data gathering issues:* When pondering if you should include demand drivers in your forecast, the first question to ask is, *"Do I have the required data?"* Many supply chains—especially manufacturers—are still small data companies, often maintaining key data in Excel files. You must weigh the pro and cons of investing in data collection and cleaning versus the expected extra forecasting insights and accuracy that this additional data will bring.

- *Non-linear effects:* Most models are still built upon linear regressions, implicitly assuming straightforward linear relationships between demand and demand drivers. But this simplistic view usually doesn't hold against data. Let's take the example of ice cream versus temperature. Obviously, the warmer the weather, the more sales you can expect. But you can't extrapolate this too much: even if it is freezing cold outside, demand won't drop to zero. (And it is unlikely clients will bring back ice cream to the stores if the temperatures drop further.) On the other hand, if it is too warm outside, people might want to avoid going out to do the groceries and stay home hydrated instead. Moreover, they can only eat so much ice cream in a single day, no matter the outside weather.

- *Cross effects between drivers:* You often need to look at a wide range of demand drivers to understand how they impact demand and how these drivers interact with each other. For example, warmer weather usually means more barbecues organized over the weekend. But the relationship isn't straightforward. For example, the first barbecues of the season might be organized despite the relatively chilly temperature—folks are just looking forward to it. In contrast, people will avoid organizing barbecues on a chilly summer evening, because they know that next weekend will enjoy better weather. But in both cases, the absolute temperature is exactly the same—it's the relative perception that is different. In this example, when forecasting demand, you should look at this weekend's temperature *and* next weekend's (which is another driver). These two temperatures will have a cross effect on today's demand.

- *Lagged effects:* Some drivers have a diffused, lagged effect. This is especially the case with marketing and advertisement. *You see an advertisement today. You buy in two weeks.* Including these drivers in a forecasting model is, therefore, especially challenging.

We have now explored both time series forecasting and the use of predictive analytics. In the next section, we will compare the two and discuss their strengths and weaknesses.

14.3 Times series forecasting vs. predictive analytics

I often conclude training sessions on statistical forecasting by asking the following questions:

- Which one is the best: time series forecasting or predictive analytics?
- Which one should you use for your supply chain?

Take a minute to think about it before turning the page. You can see a summary of the pros and cons of both approaches in table 14.2 as food for thought.

Table 14.2 Time Series vs. Predictive Analytics

Model	Complexity	Scenario planning	Data
Time series forecasting	Simple to set up	No	Limited
Predictive analytics	Requires advanced analytics	Yes	Difficult to collect

Unfortunately, there is no "overall best model" or silver bullet that would work best in 100% of cases.[47] Instead, I recommend using the following approach:

1 *Assess data availability:* There is no point in lengthy discussions about whether you should use a predictive model leveraging advanced analytics to finally discover that the underlying data is unavailable (or of very poor quality).

2 *Try out different techniques:* Try different approaches (with various models and inputs) to see how accurate they are. Putting all your eggs in the same basket is a risky bet. Especially because it is difficult (if not impossible) to assess the expected accuracy of a new model in advance. In any case, remember to compare (new) models against benchmarks (chapter 10), your current process, and your current forecasting engine.

3 *Select or combine:* If a model is a clear winner in terms of accuracy, it might be better (and simpler) only to keep this one. If multiple models end up having close accuracy, you can then average their predictions into a final single forecast. This last trick will usually deliver extra accuracy . . . at the cost of a more complicated opaque model that might confuse users.

We've briefly compared the two models, so now let's discuss now how we can practically select a model within a particular context (data, objective, metrics).

14.4   How to select a model

Creating (or selecting) a new model is not a simple task. As for any forecasting improvement journey, the 5-step framework presented in the introduction will guide you (figure 14.10).

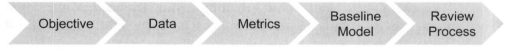

Figure 14.10   5-Step Framework for demand planning excellence

Looking at this framework, we can further detail the *baseline model* step into a 4-step virtuous loop (figure 14.11). (We will develop this loop further in chapter 15 when discussing the specificities of machine learning.)

---

[47] In general, do not to trust the hype around marketing buzzwords. Always compare forecasts against benchmarks. Do not assume that using buzzwords will improve accuracy.

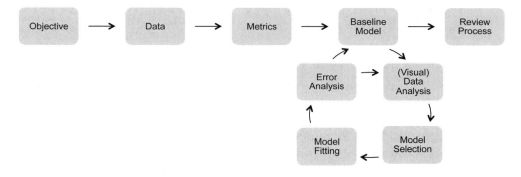

Figure 14.11   The virtuous 4-steps model creation loop

Let's take the time to revisit the first steps of the 5-step framework and the sub-steps specific to model creation.

14.4.1 *The 5-step framework*

OBJECTIVE

Before launching any forecasting improvement initiative (like creating a new model), you must assess what you need to forecast. Remember, the objective of demand forecasts is not to be accurate, but to be helpful for your supply chain to make the right decisions. To put it differently, if you are not forecasting the right thing, there is no point in improving your forecast accuracy. So, before jumping into your forecasting improvement journey, you should ensure that you are forecasting demand at the right level of aggregation (chapter 5) and over the appropriate horizon (chapter 6). Then, you can work on improving your process and model.

For example, many companies forecast demand by month by market even if they deploy inventory weekly from their plants to a few warehouses worldwide. In such a case, it makes more sense to focus on forecasting demand directly per week per warehouse. Otherwise, your colleagues will apply simplistic flat splits to cut your monthly forecasts by weeks. It would be a pity to launch a major forecasting improvement project to realize later that other teams use flat splits when deploying inventory. You need to forecast demand at the right aggregation in the first place.

DATA COLLECTION

Bad data will beat a good model—every time.

First and foremost, you need to forecast demand, not sales. See chapter 3 for more information on how to collect demand data (rather than sales).

Based on my experience with leading forecasting improvement projects, the journey's beginning is the most difficult because you need to gather and clean data without any short-term success or quick wins that would help to gain traction from management. That's why you'll need a motivated team to spend the necessary time to collect relevant data.

Beyond demand data, you might want to collect demand drivers' data as well. However, pay attention that getting some demand drivers' data might take months (and call for time-intensive work). Instead, you might want to first try a model with the data you have at hand; and improve it later with more data. Moreover, pay attention that external data bought from data providers might be expensive *and* inconsistent. For example, many providers share market information with a few months' delay based on a granularity that doesn't match your requirements. Moreover, the data provider's acquisition and cleaning process are often quite opaque: you won't be able to see obvious pitfalls. Just avoid it.

MODEL VS. PROCESS METRICS

Once the objective is clear, you must choose the right metrics to define success.

To simplify things, you could use the same metric to assess your forecasting model's quality and monitor your overall forecasting process. But, in practice, you might want to choose a set of simple KPIs to assess the process quality (as you need to communicate clear results to various teams); and choose more elaborate KPIs to evaluate your model. As discussed in Part 2, you will need to use an accuracy and a bias metric (usually, tracking bias and MAE should deliver the best compromise between business value and complexity). Moreover, if your supply chain sells products over a wide price range, you should use value-weighted metrics to account for business value (chapter 11).

I have witnessed forecasting projects fail because the metric used to assess forecasting quality by senior management wasn't aligned with business value. Unfortunately, many supply chains (and software vendors) still use obsolete forecasting metrics.[48] There is no point in running any forecasting improvement until you are sure you track the right metric.

Let's now get into the details of the four steps required to make a model.

14.4.2 *4-step model creation framework*

In this section, we will look at the four steps for creating a model (as shown in figure 14.12): (visual) data analysis, model selection, model fitting, and error analysis. Let's discuss them one by one.

---

[48] As discussed in chapters 8 and 9, an accurate unbiased forecast might result in a worse MAPE than an inaccurate biased forecast. How can you lead an improvement project under this condition?

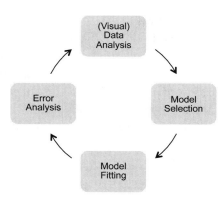

Figure 14.12   4-step model creation loop

STEP #1: (VISUAL) DATA ANALYSIS

Before jumping into the bolts and nuts of creating a new model, you must investigate demand data and drivers. One of the easiest ways to do that is to plot demand along with demand drivers (see an example in figure 14.13). Can you identify the promotions that look wrong? Look for trends, seasonality, similarities within different products/regions, impact of holidays, promotions, price changes, or any strange pattern.

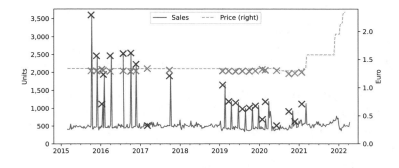

Figure 14.13   Historical demand, prices, and promotions (denoted by x marks) over time (FMCG retailer)

STEP #2: MODEL SELECTION

Choose a model that can capture the relationships identified in Step 1. Note that some advanced statistical models can capture both the demand level, trend, and seasonality *and* the impact of demand drivers (their inner workings are out of the scope of this book). In chapter 15, we will discuss machine-learning models; they are usually better at capturing multiple complicated relationships.

STEP #3: MODEL FITTING

Now that you have selected a model and have a clear objective, you can *fit* it to your dataset. Fitting a model means letting an optimization engine find the best set of parameters that fit the historical demand patterns. For example, for time series models, you will need to assess how reactive the model should be to a change of trend or seasonality. For more advanced models (such as neural networks, chapter 15), data scientists will use advanced training algorithms to optimize hidden internal parameters.

> **Pro Note**
>
> If you are currently using a forecasting software, I would advise you to challenge the vendor by asking what horizon and metrics are used to optimize the models. If you have the ability to, do not hesitate to change these metrics to align them with your requirements.

STEP #4: ERROR ANALYSIS

Fitting a model is not the end of the journey. You want to create a feedback loop by looking at your model's errors to find ways to improve it.

To do so, do not hesitate to use various graphs and visual dashboards. For example, I like to plot the most significant offender(s) to see if the model missed some obvious information (such as promotions, holidays, or shortages). Note that it makes sense to look at errors both in the training and test sets.

In case of obvious model mistakes, there are three usual possibilities:

- *The underlying data is wrong:* If your dataset includes inaccurate data, it is expected that your model won't be able to forecast demand correctly. In such a case, many planners would jump in and smooth out the outliers manually. I do not recommend doing manual data cleaning. Instead, you should find the underlying root cause and fix it.

- *Demand drivers are missing:* For example, a historical price increase impacted demand, but your model is unaware of it. So again, you cannot blame it for not forecasting demand correctly. In such a case, you must collect and clean more data and provide it to your model. Moreover, ensure that your model can leverage these new insights. As we will discuss in chapter 15, machine learning should be up to this challenge.

- *The optimization engine is not adequately set up:* Suppose the training or selection phase of the model was not done correctly (for example, because an important demand driver is not properly captured or got inadequate weights, or because the model parameters aren't adequately finetuned). In that case, you will face *overfitting* (your model spots demand patterns that are just random noise) or *underfitting* (your model does not capture actual demand patterns). In figure 14.14, you can see two extreme cases of overfitting (the model captures a seasonality, but there is none) and underfitting (the model does not capture the seasonality).

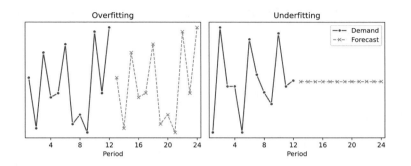

Figure 14.14   Overfitting (left) vs. underfitting (right)

This brings us to the end of the chapter. We looked at two distinct types of models: time series forecasting and predictive analysis. We then compared the two and discussed how to choose the right model for a particular situation using on the 5-step framework for demand planning excellence. Now you should be better equipped to determine the right model for your own situation!

Summary

- Statistical models are insightful because they show the interactions between historical demand, demand drivers, and the resulting forecast.

- Such models are easy to understand and interpret. Using time series forecasting, you can directly read the demand level, trend, or seasonality. If the forecast for a specific period is strange, you can investigate how the sub-components (level, trend, seasonality) or the demand drivers (pricing, promotions, etc.) are behaving to understand where the error comes from.

- Time series forecasting techniques are appreciated by supply chain practitioners (and software vendors) because they are easy to set up and do not require much data to deliver satisfactory results.

- Predictive models leverage demand drivers to forecast demand. Using these, you can analyze the impact of demand drivers (answering questions such as "*How does the weather impact demand?*") and plan scenarios ("*If I plan a promotion, future demand will increase by 15%*").

- Enriching your forecasting model with demand drivers might sound promising. But unfortunately, it is usually more challenging because you must collect clean data and manage more advanced models.

- Unfortunately, statistical models are limited by the complexity they can deal with and the accuracy they can deliver. This is where machine learning can help you move forward.

Machine learning 15

Objective ▶ Data ▶ Metrics ▶ **Baseline Model** ▶ Review Process

Tell us the things that are to come, so that we may know that you are gods.

—Isaiah 41:22

In this chapter, you will learn what machine learning is, how it works, and what you can expect when using it to forecast demand. We will also discuss pitfalls and best practices when launching an ML initiative.

If you want to learn how to create your own machine learning models, feel free to check my book, *Data Science for Supply Chain Forecasting.*

15.1   What is machine learning?

So far, we have discussed statistical models using predefined mathematical relationships to populate demand forecasts. The issue was that these models cannot adapt to demand patterns. For example, if you use a statistical model that doesn't include any seasonal factor to forecast demand for a seasonal product, it will fail to interpret the cyclical patterns. And it will likely interpret them falsely as changing trends. On the other hand, if you use a seasonal model to predict demand for a non-seasonal product, it will overfit historical random variations by interpreting them as a recurring seasonality.

Machine learning is different.

With the technological advancements of machine learning algorithms, we have new tools at our disposal that can achieve outstanding performance on typical supply chain demand datasets. These new models can learn complex relationships using historical demand and demand drivers to predict future demand.

Initially, machine learning models are just algorithmic blueprints that learn underlying relationships from datasets composed of various features. To put it differently, machine learning is about letting an algorithm understand a dataset and its underlying relationships *on its own*. You can choose the learning algorithm and its main characteristics, but you cannot explicitly control the resulting model. Technically, the algorithm will learn the relationships between data inputs and desired outputs from a *training dataset* (in our case, data inputs such as historical demand and demand drivers, and desired outputs such as future demand). Later, once trained, the algorithm can apply these relationships to new data (in our case, to predict future demand).

Whereas traditional statistical models apply predefined relationships (equations) to forecast demand, machine learning algorithms do not assume any particular relationship (like seasonality or trends) ex-ante. Instead, they will directly learn these patterns by looking at historical demand and demand drivers (figure 15.1).[49]

Figure 15.1   Statistical vs. machine-learning models

As I noted in my previous book, some could think that statistical models are already outdated and useless as machine learning models will take over thanks to their outstanding accuracy. But this is wrong: as shown in table 15.1, both

---

[49] The difference between statistical models and machine learning can sometimes be blurry. The distinction between the two can also be based on *how* the models are trained and analyzed. For example, you could set up a linear regression using a data science approach or a more traditional statistical one. In general, when referring to machine learning, I refer to tree-based models or neural networks (we will discuss these in section 14.2).

approaches have their pros and cons. Statistical models will be limited in the type of relationship they can grasp in a dataset, but they are transparent. Machine learning is the opposite.

Table 15.1 Statistical vs. Machine-Learning Models

	Statistical models	Machine learning
Explainability	White box	Black box
Complexity	Simpler	More complicated
Demand drivers	Difficult to include	Simple to include
Data requirement	Limited	Extensive
Accuracy (expected)	Lower	Higher

Artificial intelligence

Pay attention that there is no strict, clear definition of artificial intelligence (AI). On the other hand, for data scientists, it is usually clear what machine learning is or isn't. The joke goes that if it is written in Python, it is ML. And if it is written on a PowerPoint, it is AI. In general, I am very cautious of anyone pretending to do AI because this term is usually used to sell overpromising software or projects.

Note that the discussions in this chapter do not apply to linear regressions (even advanced versions such as Lasso, Ridge, and ElasticNet),[50] which I usually do not consider machine learning (even if they can technically be described as such). Some practitioners (and software vendors) present ARIMA or Prophet as machine learning. I would not agree with these statements (usually made to impress and sell projects) and classify these models as statistical ones. Instead, I include into the machine-learning umbrella models such as forests, gradient-boosted trees, and all types of neural networks

15.1.1 *How does the machine learn?*

Machine learning algorithms will run through a dataset ordered by *data features*; and (try to) pick up any underlying relationship between these data features and the desired output.[51] For example, to forecast future demand, a

---

50 More information about these models (and how to create them) is available on scikit-learn website at https://scikit-learn.org/stable/modules/linear_model.html. Scikit-learn is an amazing python library for data science and machine learning—I use it thoroughly in my book *Data Science for Supply Chain Forecasting* (Pedregosa, et al., 2011).

51 In this chapter, we will only discuss *supervised* machine learning algorithms. To simplify your reading experience, I won't mention "supervised model" or "supervised machine learning" each time. A supervised machine learning model is a model that is fed with both inputs and desired outputs. It is then up to the algorithm to understand the relationship(s) between these inputs and outputs. It is called supervised because you show the model the desired output. In other words, a supervised machine learning model learns from an existing dataset to predict outputs based on inputs. On the other hand, an *unsupervised* model is only fed with inputs and no specific desired outputs. It is then up to algorithm to categorize the different data observations. Simply put, you ask your algorithm to label each data point.

model could look at historical sales, shortages, and the weather forecast for the upcoming days.

Data feature

A data feature is a type of information a model has at its disposal to make a prediction. For example, if you want to predict tomorrow's demand using weather forecasts and recent online searches, "tomorrow's weather" and "today's number of online searches" are data features.

In table 15.2, you can see an example where the model looks at products' brands, historical demand and prices, future prices, and promotion activities to predict future demand.

Table 15.2   Typical Inputs (or Data Features) for a Machine-Learning Model

Brand	Inputs							Outputs
	Demand				Price		Promotion	Demand
	Q–4	Q–3	Q–2	Q–1	Average	Q+1	Q+1	Q+1
Low cost	1,500	500	400	300	10	10		200
Premium	500	1,000	750	500	35	30	–15%	700
Regular	250	350	150	400	20	20	–20%	300
Low cost	100	110	120	150	8	9		120
Low cost	50	30	80	10	5	5		30
Regular	200	250	220	240	15	14	–10%	260

When working on a machine learning model, you need to pay attention to two success-critical aspects:

- *The data (features) your model will use to predict future demand:* By providing relevant data to your ML model, it will be able to predict future demand more accurately because it has more insightful pieces of information at its disposal. For example, you wouldn't be able to predict the sales of a product during Black Friday without knowing if it will be on sale or not.

  You will need business insights rather than technical skills to brainstorm which features could be used. We will discuss this further in the next sub-section.

- *Fine tuning the parameters of your machine learning model:* This step requires hard skills in data science that are out of scope for this book.[52] Nevertheless, we will quickly discuss the main machine learning models in section 15.2.

FEATURE ENGINEERING

Do not leave data scientists alone when deciding what data to feed to the model. Instead, anyone with business experience should collaborate on which data features could potentially be fed to the model (this is also known as *feature engineering*).

> ### Definition: Feature engineering
> Feature engineering is the act of selecting (and creating or tweaking) data features to feed a machine learning model. (This is often seen as a technical process for data scientists. But I prefer to see it as a business process.)

To discuss which data features could be included in the model, I like to organize brainstorming sessions with various team members. To kick off the discussion, I like to ask the following question: *If I had to make a forecast for next month's demand, what questions would I ask myself? What pieces of information would I like to check?*

As you ask yourself—and your team—this question, you will get a glimpse of the most meaningful information to give to your model.

Here are a few typical answers:

- What is the current pricing of my product, and did it change over the last months?
- What is the average monthly demand for my product?
- Was the product recently out of stock?
- Are we currently running a promotion?

After gathering these questions, the difficult part begins: collecting the required data. You might have to make tradeoffs between data quality and availability. For example, you might only be able to capture some promotions—but not all. Do not freeze a data science initiative for months to gather data about a barely useful demand driver.

---

[52] For more information, see my previous book *Data Science for Supply Chain Forecasting.*

LOCAL MODELS

Traditional statistical models—such as those discussed in chapter 14—are fit independently to each product in a dataset. We call them *local models.* Simply put, if you ask a statistical model to forecast product A, it will only rely on product A's historical data alone to predict its future (and won't look at other products). This means that you can improve the accuracy of a statistical model by providing it with more historical data. (This could, for example, help with assessing monthly seasonality.) But it won't help to add new products to the dataset because the model won't apply insights learned from this new product to the other products in the dataset.

GLOBAL MODELS

In contrast, most machine learning algorithms learn patterns across an entire dataset; they are trained (or fit) using the whole dataset at once. We call these global models. In our forecasting case, global models would learn patterns using all available products' historical data (even if these patterns only apply to a subset of products). Global models will pick up various general relationships across the dataset, such as "*When I do a promotion, demand increases*" or "*If demand was growing over time in the last periods, I can expect the same trend going forward.*" One of the advantages of these models is that they should generalize well given new, unseen data. For example, even if a specific product was never promoted before, global models could transfer the learnings from other historically promoted products onto this newly promoted product.

You can increase the accuracy of global models by providing more product data giving the machine more opportunities to learn meaningful relationships. On the other hand, this also means that you cannot use machine learning on small datasets, because the algorithm won't have enough opportunities to spot meaningful relationships.

Note that using a global model doesn't always imply that the model will learn the relationships *between* products (*"If demand on product A increases, product B increases as well"*). It simply means that it will learn global properties and patterns. If you want your global model to understand interactions between products, you will need to mention them explicitly.

15.1.2 *Black boxes versus whites boxes*

Statistical models are insightful because they make explicit the interactions between input variables and predicted output(s). Such models are easy to understand and interpret (we call them *white boxes*). In chapter 14, we discussed different transparent forecasting models. Using them, you can read the level, trend, seasonality, or the impact of specific drivers (*"Promotions increase the forecast by 15%"*). Thanks to them, we can easily answer questions such as *Do we have a seasonality?* or *Is there a trend?* And if the forecast for a specific period is strange, we can look at how the sub-components (level, trend, seasonality) are behaving to understand where the error comes from.

This is unfortunately not the case with machine learning which are *black boxes.* They will never communicate to you an estimation of the level, trend, or seasonality of a product—at least not with current technologies and techniques. You won't even know if the model detects a seasonality or a trend.

OPENING THE BOX

Yet, we have two tools at our disposal to understand how a machine learning algorithm thinks: *feature importance* and *scenario analysis.*

- *Feature importance:* When using tree-based machine learning models, we can compute the importance of the data features (see an example in figure 15.2). Unfortunately, the fact that a feature such as *promotion* is important won't tell us the *impact* of running a promotion. It just means that the model pays attention to it. But we do not know *how.* Moreover, you cannot easily evaluate feature importance with neural networks. Overall, you only get limited insights from looking at the features' importance. Nevertheless, you might learn that some demand drivers are useless. For example, if you run a feature importance analysis and see that weather has a 0.01% overall importance, you know that it is not business critical.

Figure 15.2   Feature importance

Pro tip

If you see a low feature importance for a demand driver that you esteemed to be business-critical, it might indicate that the underlying data was not adequately captured, or the model was not correctly designed.

- *Scenario analysis:* You can compute the impact of demand drivers by running different forecast scenarios. For example, you could run two scenarios with and without discounts. By looking at the impact on your demand forecast, you will be able to infer the effect of running promotions (and their expected uplifts). You can see an example from a previous project in figure 15.3. The model predicts a total uplift of 17% and understands that promotions result in lower sales before and after the periods they are run in (this is called *self-cannibalization*).

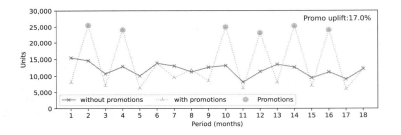

Figure 15.3   Promo uplift and scenarios

We just covered the basics of what machine learning is, some of its main characteristics, and how you can assess what's going on "under the hood". Now let's consider the main types of learning algorithms you're likely to encounter.

15.2   *Main types of learning algorithms*

In this section, we'll look at the most common learning algorithms: tree-based models and neural networks. Before jumping to these algorithms, let's briefly discuss how machine learning first emerged.

15.2.1   *Short history of machine-learning models*

Harder, Better, Faster, Stronger

—Daft Punk

Data science and machine learning models might sound modern, but the first models were conceptualized in the mid-XXth century, as illustrated in figure

15.4. The first neural network was built by Rosenblatt in 1957.[53] The same year, Holt published his work on exponential smoothing (which is still today the most widely used forecasting method).[54] Ironically, it took nearly another 30 years for damped trends to be added to exponential smoothing (now commonly used by all forecasting engines).[55] Six years later, in 1963, Morgan and Sonquist introduced the first decision tree.[56] (Even if decision trees are less known to the general public, they are the primary building block of many of the most recent models.)

So, if the first machine learning models were introduced more than 60 years ago, why didn't we hear about them earlier?

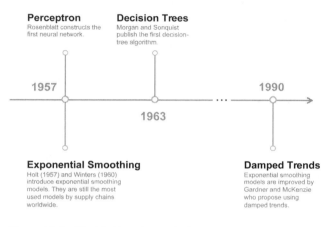

Perceptron
Rosenblatt constructs the first neural network.

Decision Trees
Morgan and Sonquist publish the first decision-tree algorithm.

1957

1990

1963

Exponential Smoothing
Holt (1957) and Winters (1960) introduce exponential smoothing models. They are still the most used models by supply chains worldwide.

Damped Trends
Exponential smoothing models are improved by Gardner and McKenzie who propose using damped trends.

Figure 15.4   Machine learning early days

Four elements explain this:

- *Computation power:* Computation power is growing at an exponential rate. The 2019 iPhone had 100,000 times faster processing speed than 1969 Apollo 11 (and one to ten million times more memory).[57]
- *Data:* Businesses also have more data at hand today than yesterday (especially retailers and e-retailers).

---

[53] Rosenblatt, 1957.
[54] Winters, 1960. Holt, 2004.
[55] Gardner, et al., 1985.
[56] Morgan, et al., 1963.
[57] See the article "The first moon landing was achieved with less computing power than a cell phone or a calculator" by Graham Kendall. Pacific Standard, 2019. Available at https://psmag.com/social-justice/ground-control-to-major-tim-cook

These first two reasons are often used to explain the rise of machine learning. But they don't explain everything. We already had plenty of data in 2010 and enough computation power to run machine-learning models.

Two other trends explain the recent rise of machine learning:

- *Powerful efficient algorithms:* Over time, while the scientific community was developing more powerful machine-learning algorithms, computer scientists perfected their software implementations—making models much faster to run. For example, neural networks benefited from multiple drastic improvements between 2010 and 2015. Likewise, tree-based methods have also enjoyed numerous breakthroughs since 2015.
- *Simplicity:* As machine learning takes over the world, the tools to implement these models are becoming simpler, and—thanks to a variety of resources—it is now easier than ever to learn how to code and apply data science best practices.[58]

Simply put, in 2015, you wouldn't have had the required algorithms to achieve good enough forecasting accuracy. Before 2010, implementing any machine learning model would have been a challenge.

What is especially striking with machine learning is its continuous growth: faster, smarter algorithms are still developed and released every year by the scientific community. On the other hand, I do not expect much from *new* statistical models.

Let's discuss the two main types of machine-learning models currently used to forecast demand.

Note to the reader

The following two sections about machine-learning models are more detailed and technical. They are presented as extra material. If you are not interested in such details, feel free to skip to the next section.

15.2.2   *Tree-based models*

As explained in my book, *Data Science for Supply Chain Forecasting*, decision trees are a class of machine learning algorithms that create a map (a tree) of questions to make a prediction. This map is created based on a dataset—that's why we say that the machine learns.

---

[58] For example, in my book *Data Science for Supply Chain Forecasting*, I implement a neural network to forecast demand in only 60 lines of code (mostly data formatting).

To make a prediction, a decision tree will ask a series of simple yes/no questions until it gets to a final prediction. For example, *will you run a promotion next month? Did you sell more than ten units last month? Did the price increase since last quarter?* Somehow you might see these trees as a giant game of the famous '80s game "Guess Who?".

Technically, each question is called a *node* (for example, in figure 15.5, the question *"Does the person have a big nose?"* is a node). And each possible final answer (prediction) is called a *leaf.* In figure 15.5, each leaf contains only one person, which is not mandatory. You could imagine multiple people having a big mouth and a big nose.

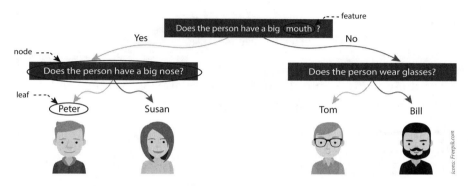

Figure 15.5   A decision tree applied to the game "Guess Who?"

Without going too much into detail, the algorithm that grows trees will run through nodes by asking questions (technically, we say that it *performs a split*) about available features. When splitting a node, the algorithm will choose the best possible question by minimizing prediction error across the two resulting data subsets (leaves). Simply put, you want to ask relevant questions that divide heterogeneous observations into two smaller subsets that would be as homogenous as possible. Here is an example using "Guess Who?". A relevant question would be: *"Does the person have a big mouth?"* because it would divide the four characters into two subgroups. On the other hand, a question such as *"Does the person wear clothes?"* wouldn't bring any insights as they all have clothes.

Let's illustrate how trees work with a typical supply chain forecasting dataset. Let's imagine that you trained your model on a dataset such as illustrated in table 15.3.

Table 15.3   Typical Inputs (or Data Features) for a Machine-Learning Model

Brand	Inputs							Outputs
	Demand				Price		Promotion	Demand
	Q–4	Q–3	Q–2	Q–1	Average	Q+1	Q+1	Q+1
Low cost	1,500	500	400	300	10	10		200
Premium	500	1,000	750	500	35	30	–15%	700
Regular	250	350	150	400	20	20	–20%	300
Low cost	100	110	120	150	8	9		120
Low cost	50	30	80	10	5	5		30
Regular	200	250	220	240	15	14	–10%	260

Using these features and the underlying relationships it learned, a tree could ask the following yes/no questions to make a prediction:

- Is *demand Q–1* > 300?
- Yes
- Is *average price* > 20?
- No
- Is *price Q+1* < 25?
- No
- Prediction = 550.

A SHORT HISTORY OF TREE-BASED MODELS

The initial implementation of a decision tree was proposed more than 60 years ago by Morgan and Sonquist (figure 15.6). Even though recent decision tree implementations are still based on yes/no questions, they are (much) more powerful than the initial model.[59] Modern versions leverage hundreds of (simple) trees specialized in predicting the previously created trees' mistakes. In simple words, the algorithm populates hundreds of trees one by one, where each new tree pays more attention to what the previous trees got wrong. This approach is called *boosting* and was imagined first in the 90s. The most recent implementations (light gradient boosting and extreme gradient boosting) can deliver lightning-fast stellar results.[60]

---

[59] Freund and Schapire published in 1997 with their AdaBoost model (for Adaptive Boosting), the algorithmic foundation of the following boosting models. Freund, et al., 1997.

[60] See *XGBoost* by Tianqi Chen and Carlos Guestrin (2016) and *LightGBM* by Guolin Ke and his team (2017). Chen, et al., 2016. Ke, et al., 2017.

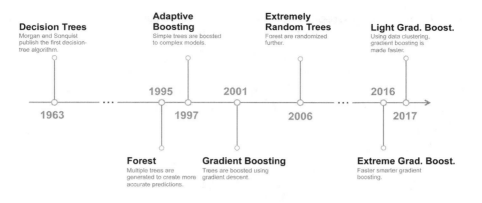

Figure 15.6   Decision trees over time

The *Forest* algorithm is also widely known: it averages the predictions of hundreds of independent trees. This technique is famous as it is simpler to use than the newer boosted approaches and usually gets decent results.

15.2.3 *Neural networks*

An (artificial) neural network is a network of neurons using mathematical functions to gather insights from different inputs (usually previous neurons) to generate a numerical output (often used by other neurons as an input). A neural network (composed of layers of neurons) is trained using a specific optimization algorithm. Let's explain each of these terms.

As illustrated in figure 15.7, an (artificial) neuron is a (mathematical) cell receiving numerical information from various inputs. The neuron then applies a mathematical function (called the *activation function*) to process these inputs and generate a (numerical) output. In practice, each neuron allocates different weights (importance) to each input and then applies its activation function. Do not imagine anything complicated for the activation function; it is usually something similar to a capped weighted sum.

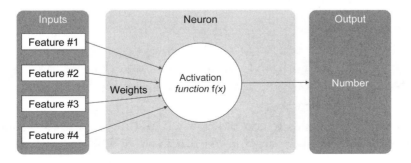

Figure 15.7   Artificial neuron

Simply put, a neuron transforms (numerical) inputs into an output using an activation function. And choosing the activation function is critical because it determines the neurons' behavior.

Now that we know how a neuron and an activation function work, let's look at how neural networks work.[61] As shown in figure 15.8, a neural network is composed of three types of layers: one *input layer*, multiple *hidden layers*, and finally, one *output layer* (with the data flowing from one layer to the next, this is called *forward propagation*).

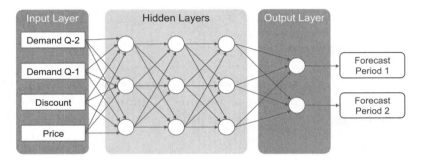

Figure 15.8   Artificial neural network

- *Input layer:* This layer passes the input features to the first hidden layer. In figure 15.7, I illustrate this using four features).

- *Hidden layers:* These layers are the neural network's core. This is where the magic happens: the neural network gets insights as its processes inputs using activations functions and weights. Therefore, designing the shape of the hidden layers (number of layers and neurons per layer) is a critical task for data scientists.

- *Output layer:* This is the final layer. Each neuron corresponds to a prediction. For example, in figure 15.8, one neuron corresponds to the forecast for Period 1, and the second neuron the forecast for Period 2.

OPTIMIZATION AND TRAINING

When data scientists say they *train* (or *fit*) a neural network, it means that they are using an advanced algorithm to optimize the network's inner weights (represented by the arrows between the neurons in figures 15.7 and 15.8).

A SHORT HISTORY OF NEURAL NETWORKS

Artificial neurons date back to the 1940s, when McCulloch and Pitts modeled the biological working of an organic neuron to show how simple units could

---

[61] I describe here one specific type of neural network called *feedforward neural network*. Also, I use some shortcuts for the sake of simplicity and clarity (for example, neurons usually use biases in their activation functions).

replicate logical functions (figure 15.9). In the 1950s, Rosenblatt created the *Perceptron*, a massive machine containing a single layer of neurons. This electrical device could classify rudimentary pictures of digits and be trained automatically based on a dataset. For the training algorithm, Rosenblatt inspired himself from the work of the Canadian psychologist Donald Hebb, who theorized in 1949 that connections between (organic) neurons are reinforced as they are used. *The New York Times* reported Rosenblatt prophesizing that Perceptrons would in the future be able to "recognize people and call out their name," "instantly translate speech in one language to speech or writing in another language," "be fired to the planets as mechanical space explorers," but also "reproduce itself," and be self-conscious. Unfortunately, due to its training algorithm, the Perceptron was limited to a single layer of neurons, which is insufficient to capture complex relationships. This limitation resulted in the first *neural network winter* until the mid-1980s.

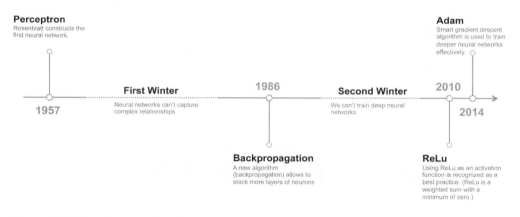

Figure 15.9   Neural network timeline

In the mid-1980s, academics popularized a new algorithm *(backpropagation)* to optimize neural networks, allowing the training of neural networks with multiple neuron layers.[62] These deeper networks were up to more complicated tasks such as handwriting recognition.[63] Unfortunately, backpropagation alone wasn't sufficient to train deep networks effectively and efficiently. Once again, the research community lost interest in neural networks. In the late 2000s, multiple new algorithms were popularized (such as the optimization method *Adam* and the *ReLu* activation function; see figure 15.9). They resulted in faster, more stable optimization, enabling the training of much deeper neural networks.

---

[62] Paul Werbos was the first to propose using backpropagation to optimize neural networks in his 1974 PhD thesis. The use of backpropagation was popularized later by the work of Rumelhart (1986). Werbos, 1974. Rumelhart, et al., 1986.

[63] LeCun, et al., 1989.

15.3   *What should you expect from ML-driven demand forecasting?*

When it comes to forecasting using machine-learning models, many companies (and individuals) expect too much or too little. When launching an ML initiative, if you expect and promise too much, top management will get frustrated when predictions inevitably underdeliver. Moreover, demand planners will become cautious and reluctant to use an overpromised tool (that will unavoidably commit mistakes). On the other hand, if you expect too little from ML, you will miss the opportunity to launch a data science initiative that might have a high ROI.

So, how much can you expect from machine learning?

15.3.1   *Forecasting competitions*

The international forecasting community organizes competitions every year (some specifically focusing on retail demand forecasting).[64] These competitions help to understand the current state-of-the-art and assess the added value of edge models compared to benchmarks. (As discussed in chapter 10, comparing a model to a benchmark is the best way to determine its added value.)

Since 2018, three competitions have been organized specifically on retail demand forecasting (see a short description in table 15.4).

Table 15.4   Retail Forecasting Competitions Since 2018

Competition	Year	Granularity	Forecast-items	Horizon	Data
Corporacion Favorita[65]	2018	Store x Product x Day	210,000	16 days	4.5 years of sales, price ranges, and promotions
M5 (Walmart)[66]	2020	Store x Product x Day	42,840	42 days	4 years of sales and pricing
Intermarché	2021	Store x Product x Day	275,781	90 days	1 year of sales and price ranges

---

[64] Mostly thanks to Spyros Makridakis' leadership who organized 6 competitions since 1979. You can read his story at https://robjhyndman.com/hyndsight/forecasting-competitions/. Hyndman, 2018.

[65] See *Learnings from Kaggle's Forecasting Competitions* by Casper Solheim Bojer and Jens Peder Meldgaard. This article is freely available on arxiv. Bojer, et al., 2021.

[66] See *The M5 Accuracy competition: Results, findings and conclusions* by Spyros Makridakis, Evangelos Spiliotis, and Vassilis Assimakopoulos. It is freely available at https://www.researchgate.net/publication/344487258_The_M5_Accuracy_competition_Results_findings_and_conclusions. Makridakis, et al., 2022.

All of them have been won by machine learning. Actually, all the top participants used machine learning-driven models. You can see the winning results compared to benchmarks in table 15.5. Unfortunately, each competition tracked a different accuracy metric (often quite elaborate and specific) and used another benchmark, making any added value comparison difficult. Nevertheless, the resulting forecast error reductions can give you an idea of the expected improvement range that advanced models could bring.

Table 15.5   Forecasting Competitions: Models vs. Benchmarks. (The Benchmark for Intermarché Is Based on my Own Results.)

Competition	Year	Metric	Benchmark (Model)	Benchmark (Score)	Winning model (Score)	Improvement
Corporación Favorita	2018	Normalized Weighted Root Mean Squared Logarithmic Error (NWRMSLE)	Seasonal naive	0.8486	0.5092	60.0%
M5	2020	Weighted Root Mean Squared Scaled Error (WRMSSE)	Exponential smoothing	0.6710	0.5204	22.4%
Intermarché	2021	Root Mean Squared Logarithmic Error (RMSLE)	Seasonal moving average	0.6088	0.5478	10.0%

As you can see in table 15.5, Corporación Favorita enjoys a massive improvement. But this is likely due to the benchmark used: a simplistic seasonal naïve forecast. On the other hand, Intermarché displays a modest gain of 10%. But, again, this is likely due to the metric used (logarithmic squared error) and the lack of historical data (a single year was provided).[67]

Based on my experience as a supply chain data scientist, usual machine-learning projects result in a forecast error reduction ranging from 0% to 33% compared to moving averages. This accuracy improvement will be more significant as more data is available (such as historical shortages, promotions, and pricing). Promotions alone can be responsible for a gain of up to 15%. Machine learning is also generally better at forecasting granular demand as more data is available.

---

[67] See the interview "How to win a Forecasting Competition?" I published with four of the winners of the competition (freely available at https://youtube.com/watch?v=kkpFZA1sVSA).

On the other hand, I have personally witnessed many companies (software and consultants alike) overselling demand forecasting projects and expected results. When presented with extreme results or promises, we must watch for fallacies in data and metrics. It is very easy to manipulate data to show improvement.[68] If it seems too good to be true, it probably is.

15.3.2 *Improving the baseline*

Machine-learning models are likely to beat statistical models. But they might fail to beat your current overall forecasting process. This is normal. As we will discuss in chapter 16, demand planners can usually deliver accurate forecasts using information that models are unaware of. For example, planners can communicate with their clients—something ML can't do (yet).

On the other hand, using advanced models will improve your forecasting baseline accuracy. By doing so, your demand planning team will be able to focus on the few remaining products that the model can't predict (such as new products). Or on the products for which they have specific insights (we will discuss this further in chapter 16). As your team edits the ML-made forecasts, you will improve the accuracy of the overall forecasting process. Usually, a more accurate model will also reduce your team workload.

For example (as displayed in table 15.6), let's imagine your current forecast engine reaches an error of 45% and that your team can usually reduce it to 41% thanks to their work. By updating the model and using machine learning, you can reach a baseline accuracy of 41%. Then your team should be able to raise it further to 39%.

Table 15.6 Example of FVA analysis with and without a ML model

Before					After				
Step	MAE	FVA	Bias	FVA	Step	MAE	FVA	Bias	FVA
Benchmark	52%		−1%		Benchmark	52%		−1%	
Baseline model	45%	+7	−3%	−2	ML model	41%	+11	−2%	−1
Demand planners	41%	+4	1%	+2	Demand planners	39%	+2	1%	+1

---

[68] I once witnessed a consultancy company presenting outstanding accuracy results to a shared client. Their Power-Point contained a footnote where one could read, «Results obtained by removing the 5% worst forecast errors».

In short, machine-learning models won't make your demand planning team obsolete. Instead, they will reduce their workload and help them to achieve better overall accuracy.

15.4 *How to launch a machine-learning initiative*

Your roadmap for leading a machine learning initiative should be based on the *5-step model creation framework* introduced in chapter 14. As illustrated in figure 15.10, we can slightly update it by segregating the *Model Fitting* step into two different steps: *feature selection* and *parameter optimization* (we discussed both aspects in section 15.1.2).

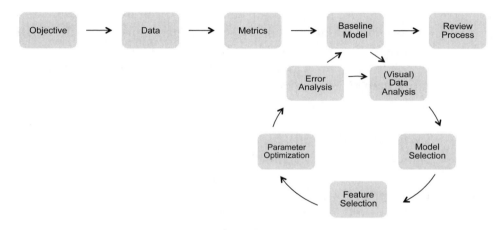

Figure 15.10   Step model creation framework adapted for machine learning

Furthermore, you need to pay attention to the following four pitfalls:

- *Testing setup:* The only proper way to assess a model forecasting quality is to test it against historical periods that weren't used to select data features or optimize the parameters. (This left-over dataset is usually called a *test set* by data scientists.) For example, you could use 2018-2022 demand data to select, fine-tune, and optimize your model. And use 2023 data to assess its accuracy. A usual mistake would be to use the same year (or historical timespan) to choose the best model among a pool of contenders *and* showcase the best results as the outcome of your project; this cherry-picking would be cheating. Finally, always remember to compare the accuracy achieved by your model against a simple benchmark (chapter 10), your current forecasting engine, and your consensus forecast. When doing so, compare the results over the same periods and granularity level. You need to compare apples with apples.

- *Why vs. what:* Many projects fail because data scientists jump on using the latest in-fashion models without consideration for the actual business needs (forecasting granularity and horizon—see chapters 5 and 6). They might also track inappropriate metrics (such as MAPE or overlooking the bias—Part 2) or data (sales vs. demand—chapter 2). Before launching any initiative, take the time to set the right objective, collect the right data, and use the right metric. In short, follow the *5-steps model creation framework.*

- *Get expectations right:* As discussed earlier, promise too much and you will disappoint and face end-users' resistance. Promise too little, and the project won't get traction. Machine learning can reduce the forecast error by 0 to 30% compared to a benchmark. You can easily beat benchmarks by more than 15% using demand drivers such as promotions or pricing. But do not expect more than a 30% forecast error reduction (except if you start from an incredibly immature process or if some demand drivers massively impact demand).

- *Infinite possibilities:* Machine learning is not a single monolithic approach. There are tens (hundreds?) of different models—new ones are published every year. Moreover, each model has various ways to be set up thanks to different data architectures and parameters. It is not because an ML initiative failed in the past that ML will never work for you. Assuming this would be like saying, *"We used math before, and it didn't work. Math will never work for us."*

This brings us to the end of the chapter. We've discussed the fundamentals of machine learning, the main learning models and their histories, and we've gone over what your expectations should be from ML-powered demand forecasting, as well as how you might launch a machine learning initiative in your own workplace. I hope this will go some way in encouraging you to explore the applications of machine learning for yourself.

Summary

- Machine-learning models can leverage various demand drivers to provide unprecedented forecasting accuracy.

- Thanks to its accuracy, a forecast baseline generated by machine learning will reduce your team's workload and deliver accurate forecasts, bringing you closer to true *demand forecasting excellence.*

- On the other side, these models are black boxes—even if you can generate helpful demand scenarios.
- To lead your machine-learning initiative, take the time to properly assess your objective, metrics, and data (following the 5-step framework for demand planning excellence). Then use the usual data science best practices to create a customized model to your needs and dataset.

Judgmental forecasting

In chapters 14 and 15, we discussed how forecasting models work. Forecasting engines will populate a forecast baseline, but this is not the end of your forecasting process. As illustrated in figure 16.1, different teams can still enrich the forecast using various insights and sources of information. Because they rely on human judgment, these adjustments are called *judgmental forecasts.*

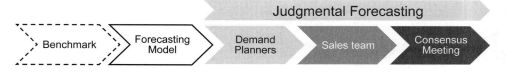

Figure 16.1 Example of a demand planning process

As we will discuss in this chapter, judgmental forecasts come with risks and pitfalls. Nevertheless, if done correctly, they should add great value to your forecasts.[69]

First and foremost, tracking forecast value added (chapter 12) is the cornerstone of any demand planning process using judgmental forecasts. You *absolutely* need to implement it to enforce ownership and accountability for all stakeholders participating in the demand planning process. Tracking added value will help you to monitor your process, but looking at this metric alone won't provide advice or guidelines on *how* to edit the forecast or *why* some colleagues struggle to add value. This is what this chapter is about.

16.1 When to use judgmental forecasts?

Let's start by asking ourselves a general question: In which case should planners use their own judgments to edit the forecast baseline?

In general, using judgmental forecasts is a good idea *if* you can leverage information your forecasting model is unaware of. Here are a few good and bad examples:

- *"I know that my main client expects lower sales than usual. I will reduce the forecast."*
  This sounds like a good idea, because it is unlikely your model is in direct contact with your clients.

- *"I will manually create the forecast for this new product."*
  This is a good idea. Taking care of new products is usually one of the main tasks of demand planners, because forecasting models (usually) can't accurately predict the demand for new products.

- *"We will increase pricing next month. I should reduce future forecasts."*
  If your forecasting model doesn't consider pricing, it is a good idea to update the forecast manually (see section 14.2.1 for a discussion about including prices in a forecasting model.). If your model uses pricing as a feature, this doesn't sound like a good idea to enrich this forecast (because the model is already aware of a price change).

- *"I think the trend for this product should be higher."*
  Forecasting models usually pick up trends on their own. If you do not have more information about this product, it is uncertain if you'll be

---

[69] For more detailed discussions, ideas, and best practices, see the books *Superforecasting: The Art and Science of Prediction* by Philip E. Tetlock and Dan Gardner (Broadway Books, 2016) and *The Business Forecasting Deal* by Michael Gilliland (John Wiley & Sons, 2010), or the article "Managing functional biases in organizational forecasts" by Rogelio Oliva and Noel Watson, *Production and Operations Management*, 2009. Oliva, et al., 2009. Tetlock, et al., 2016. Gilliland, 2010.

able to beat the forecasting model. And if your model doesn't pick up an obvious pattern (such as a trend or a seasonality), you should fix the root cause rather than spend time editing every forecast manually. Remember, demand forecasting excellence is based on efficacy and efficiency: we want to work less and let our forecast engine do the heavy lifting.

- "I think this product's seasonality should be different."
  Your forecasting model should be able to pick up seasonality correctly. If there is an obvious mistake, it might make more sense to improve your model (or change your forecasting engine) rather than correct each product manually.

- "We expect a massive change in the market condition next month. I will update the forecast."
  It is unlikely that your model is aware of this situation, so it might be a good idea to review your forecast.

- "There was a special event last month. I need to correct historical demand manually."
  Rather than manually editing historical figures, it might be safer to tag specific events on such historical periods and let the model handle them (assuming your forecasting engine can deal with specific events).

- Judgmental forecasts are also appropriate to forecast products when you lack historical data or when significant changes are ongoing (due to changing client behavior, new competition, changing legislation, a global pandemic or war, etc.).

Obviously, these situations are not always black and white. You could beat a forecast model using your judgment even if you do not have access to any particular insight. And a forecasting model could beat you even if you have access to extra information.

Nevertheless, we can generalize the previous examples by saying that the best practice should be to only update forecasts if you have insights at your disposal that your model is not aware of. By following this rule, you ensure that your team saves time by working on the products where they are the most likely to add value. Remember, we have two objectives for our demand planning process: efficacy and efficiency. So, you do not want your teams to review every forecast; instead, they need to *focus* on where they are more likely to add value.

Pro tip

Looking at the adjustments your team usually makes will help you understand your model's limitations and whether it might make sense to improve it. For example, if your team can easily beat your model without having access to extra information, it means that your model isn't good enough. If your team is spending time forecasting promotions, it might be time to include promotions as a demand driver in your model. If your team needs to review all seasonal items, it might mean that your model isn't good enough at spotting seasonal patterns.

16.2 Judgmental biases

Judgmental forecasts are prone to various biases intrinsic to how our business organizations and human brains work. As shown in figure 16.2, we can map the sources of judgmental biases into *cognitive biases, intentional biases* (primarily due to misalignment of incentives), and *biased processes.*[70]

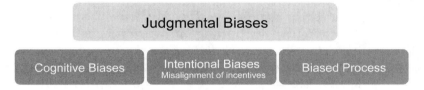

Figure 16.2   Sources of judgmental biases

Before discussing these sources further, let's remember what a demand forecast is (the best-unbiased estimate of a business' future unconstrainted demand) and what a demand forecast is not (a financial budget, a sales target to incentivize sales representatives, or a production/supply plan).

16.2.1 Cognitive biases

As humans, we are all prone to a collection of cognitive biases due to our inner brain nature. These cognitive biases, resulting from generations of evolution, are deeply embedded in our reasoning—hardwired in our brains. These biases most likely made us very good hunter-gatherers, but they also often make us reliably poor forecasters. Being conscious of these shortcomings can help us avoid them.

---

[70] Rogelio Oliva and Noel Watson proposed a framework dividing biases between intentional and unintentional in their article "Managing Functional Biases in Organizational Forecasts: A Case Study of Consensus Forecasting in Supply Chain Planning," *Production and Operations Management,* Oliva, et al., 2009.

John Mello described in details possible sources of intentional biases in his article "The Impact of Sales Forecast Game Playing on Supply Chains," Mello, Foresight Spring, 2009.

Let's review the main cognitive biases that are the most likely to deteriorate the quality of our forecasts.

ANCHORING BIAS

Humans think by comparison. When making a prediction (or an estimate), the first number we think of—even if unrelated to the task—will impact our guess. This was observed in 1974 in an experiment by Tversky and Kahneman.[71] In their experiment, they asked participants to guess the number of African countries in the UN. They showed that participants' guesses were influenced by numbers given by spinning a wheel of fortune. If a prediction can be influenced so easily by something as uncorrelated to the task as a wheel of fortune, imagine the impact when a team member starts a meeting by saying, "*I believe we will sell 20% more than last quarter*". We call this effect *anchoring*: the first number that comes to mind will anchor the discussion. For example, anchoring is also often used in negotiations to anchor the conversation from the start around a high or low number.

CONFIRMATION BIAS

Humans are also prone to *confirmation bias*. We *unconsciously* look for (and pay attention to) information supporting our current beliefs and ideas while avoiding contradictory information.[72] "*I think this product launch will be great. In one interview, one potential client said she loved it.*" Humans will also need more supporting evidence to accept any theory that would contradict their current beliefs.

Let's apply this to forecasting. Imagine you are currently thinking that next month is going to be a good month. When looking for information about next month's sales, you will (unconsciously) prefer evidence supporting the idea that your company will do great. Confirmation bias is often reinforced by the fact that we tend to look for information supporting what we want or have an interest in believing (you *wish* your company sales grew). Moreover, we also tend to stick with like-minded people. As a final example, marketing people might lean to over forecast the expected sales uplift of their upcoming campaign due to both intentional and unintentional biases. They are surrounded by other like-minded marketing professionals, prone to confirmation bias (they are likely to look more at information supporting the value of their campaign rather than disproving it) and have a direct interest in communicating the

---

[71] For more information about the anchoring bias, you can read Anchoring Effect by David McRaney (You Are Not So Smart, 2010, https://youarenotsosmart.com/2010/07/27/anchoring-effect), 2010.

[72] If you wish to learn more about cognitive biases, see the article "On the failure to eliminate hypotheses in a conceptual task" by Peter Wason, SAGE Publications, 1960, for one of the first analyses of confirmation bias. Or the more recent online article "Confirmation bias: believing what you see, seeing what you believe" by Anne-Laure Le Cunff (https://nesslabs.com/confirmation-bias), Wason, 1960; Le Cunff, 2019.

idea of a successful campaign to secure funding. (Moreover, demand planners might have difficulties contradicting this enthusiasm not to appear rude or demotivated.)

APOPHENIA AND HINDSIGHT

The human brain is hardwired to see patterns in the noise and find causes and explanations for every consequence. This effect is called apophenia: our brains look for patterns everywhere.[73] In a forecasting process, this might materialize in two ways:

- We will spot patterns when looking at graphs depicting historical demand—even if it is noisy and random. This might increase our confidence in our judgmental forecasting abilities.

- We will want to explain every single up and down in sales. Unfortunately, some businesses like to report on every historical demand/forecast deviation, when part of it is due to random variations.

Along with apophenia comes the hindsight bias, which can be described as the "*I knew it all along*" phenomenon. There is a common tendency for people to see past events as more predictable than they were. Typically, after a specific event (global pandemic, war, politics), many will think that they could have (or they did) predict it with a high level of certainty.

To improve your forecasts, rather than looking at explaining wrong historical predictions ("*What did we miss last month?*") or arguing who was right or wrong ("*I knew it all along!*"), focus on removing intentional and unintentional biases and including new sources of information (people and data alike) covering previous blind spots ("*How can we make sure we do not miss this information next time?*").

16.2.2 *Misalignment of incentives (intentional biases)*

Imagine you are sitting at your monthly S&OP consensus meeting discussing next month's forecast. As illustrated in figure 16.3, a sales representative, the customer service manager, and a finance manager sit in the room. Leading the meeting, you ask them their opinion about next month's forecast:

- "*We will sell 500 pieces*", says the sales representative.

- "*I would bet on 2,000 pieces*", says the customer service manager.

- "*Actually, my number shows that we should sell 1,250 pieces*", concludes the finance manager.

Can you trust their forecasts?

---

[73] The term was coined by psychiatrist Klaus Conrad in his 1958 publication on the early stages of schizophrenia "Die beginnende Schizophrenie," Conrad, *Thieme Verlag*, 1958.

Figure 16.3   Discussing the forecast with your team

Different supply chain stakeholders have different objectives and incentives. They might have a direct interest in increasing or decreasing forecasts (irrespective of what they expect the demand to be). Due to this misalignment, some might *intentionally* bias their forecasts (figure 16.4).

Figure 16.4   Stakeholders and their intentionally biased forecasts

In our earlier example (figure 16.3):

- The sales representative will be rewarded if she oversells compared to the forecast. So, she has an interest in reducing the forecast to get lower sales targets. This is called *sandbagging*.
- On the other hand, customer service wants to secure enough inventory to be sure to satisfy all client orders—their main KPI. Therefore, they will over forecast demand to be on the safe side. This is called *hedging*. (Some teams might also want to push some specific products forward. Think about a project manager advocating for her new product. This will also result in over forecasts.)
- Finally, to continue with our example, management and finance will pressure the demand planning team to match the yearly budget in their forecasts—this is common if the company is currently underselling compared to the budget. This is often called *enforcing*.

These examples are just a few illustrations of the many possible cases. Based on your supply chain incentives schemes (or HR policies) and culture, you might face different teams pushing the forecast in different directions. Here are another few examples:[74]

- *Enforcing:* In case of declining sales, salespeople might increase the forecast to align it with the budget not to lose face to higher management.
- *Hedging:* Salespeople might intentionally over forecast to ensure stock availabilities for opportunistic sales.
- Regional demand planners might be pressured by their local managers to increase their forecasts to secure constrained supply from a central warehouse. For example, suppose you heard that your company's global production plant is about to face a supply issue on some of your highest-margin products. You will react by increasing the demand forecast of your local market, hoping that this will trigger a deployment order for you to get the remaining global stock (before the other markets). (As discussed in chapter 4, this behavior will result in self-fulfilling prophecies and in a terrible bullwhip effect.)

In general, people who have an interest (due to their bonus scheme, KPIs, or politics) in having an optimistic or pessimistic forecast are likely to produce one (even unintentionally, as we will discuss in section 16.2.3). This is especially

---

[74] For more examples, see *The Impact of Sales Forecast Game Playing on Supply Chains* by John Mello, Foresight, 2009.

the case if they aren't held responsible for the achieved accuracy (in particular, if you do not track forecast value added, as explained in chapter 12).

16.2.3 *Biased forecasting process*

Just as humans can be biased, your demand planning process can also be biased due to one-sided data or assumptions, selective justifications, or an imbalance in stakeholders' influence.

ONE-SIDED DATA OR ASSUMPTIONS

A forecast might result in an over- or under-pessimistic estimation of future demand as it relies on partial, biased, or incomplete information. For example, your forecasting process might emphasize looking at the number of store closures rather than openings, product launches rather than discontinuations, marketing efforts rather than competitors' actions, and so on. By only looking at some figures or only including in the process stakeholders that bring a specific type of information to the table, you might create blind spots in the forecasting process.

> **Attention point**
>
> The most common case of an informational blind spot is to look at historical sales rather than demand, because most supply chains only keep track of constrained sales. Only looking at sales data without including the number of lost sales will invariably result in biased information. Collecting lost sales in a B2C environment can be particularly tricky, if not impossible. Yet, any progress toward collecting data about lost sales will help you to get an unbiased demand forecast. B2B usually provides more information as these businesses can usually collect lost orders from their clients. See chapters 3 and 4 for more information.

SELECTIVE JUSTIFICATIONS

The overall forecasting process can also be biased due to an unbalanced need to explain specific forecast adjustments (or justify forecast errors ex-ante). For example, if senior management asks for detailed justifications for any downward forecasts—but welcomes positive adjustments without much questioning—it will lead to frequent over forecasts. On the other hand, if the S&OP process asks to justify all historical over forecasts, planners will soon become conservative.

Pro tip: Avoiding over- and under-forecasting?

As noted in chapter 8, supply chains often face the temptation to value positive and negative forecast errors differently as they might have a business incentive to avoid over- or under-forecasts. As discussed in my book *Inventory Optimizations: Models and Simulations*, the cost of having one product too many (extra holding costs or spoilage) or one product too few (unhappy clients, lost revenues) is not the same. Nevertheless, by trying to avoid over- or under-forecasts, you will get biased forecasts. This will, in turn, gradually reduce confidence in the overall forecasting process . . . . Until other teams and planners start creating their own projections because they do not trust the official demand forecast anymore. Remember, a demand forecast is an unbiased unconstrained prediction of future demand; this is not a supply plan or a sales target (see chapter 2). It is always better to balance the risk of over-forecasting and under-forecasting each product by setting proper service level targets and allocating the right amount of safety stocks. This should be left to inventory planners and their optimization engine.

IMBALANCE IN STAKEHOLDERS' INFLUENCE

Finally, suppose that a stakeholder (such as a specific channel manager, a factory manager, or the sales team as a whole) has more power or influence than others. In that case, they can influence the forecast to suit their needs, multiplying the impact of misalignment of incentives. This influence can be due to personal relationships, charisma, or the fluctuating interest of senior management in forecasting. If the loudest team member in the room heavily influences the forecast, you might be facing this issue. Note that power and influence are also driven by who has access to the appropriate information and, in the end, by the last person who will sign off the forecast. This issue is often faced when executives do not want to sign off a forecast showing declining sales or that they are not meeting current sales targets.

16.3 *Group forecasts*

Instead of relying on one person to make a prediction—we just saw that we all suffer from cognitive biases and limited information—you can leverage the intelligence of multiple team members. By involving various people, you implicitly hope their biases and information sources will be different and complementary.

As we will discuss, combining the predictions of many different individuals is expected, on average, to result in a better prediction than any individual forecast. But these collective forecasts also come with pitfalls—you will have to follow a set of best practices to reap the full benefits.

16.3.1 *Wisdom of the crowds*

In 1906 Francis Galton, an 84-year-old English scientist, visited a livestock fair.[75] He witnessed a contest: villagers were invited to guess the weight of an ox. Eight hundred people participated in this contest, noting their guesses on tickets.

> *The hope of a prize and the joy of competition prompted each competitor to do his best. The competitors included butchers and farmers, some of whom were highly expert in judging the cattle weight.*
>
> —Frances Galton (1906)

After the event, Galton performed a statistical analysis of the various guesses. To his surprise, averaging all the guesses resulted in a virtually perfect weight estimation—beating the actual winner of the contest and the guesses made by all the experts.

This specific finding can be generalized as the principle that the average opinion of a group of people is expected to be more precise (on average) than the opinion of a single group member.[76] (Under some conditions, as discussed in the following sections.) This concept was coined and formalized much later in 2004 as *the wisdom of the crowds* and by James Surowiecki in his eponymous book.

The wisdom of the crowd—*gathering different people's opinions to get a better prediction*—works in most situations. From judgmental demand forecasts to predicting the outcome of any situation—professional or personal.

But this wisdom is not guaranteed; for it to emerge out of a crowd, you need three main elements (figure 16.5):[77]

- Objective alignment
- Mindset diversity
- Independence of work and judgment

---

[75] As told in the book *The Wisdom of Crowds* by James Surowiecki, Anchor, 2005, and the article "Revisiting Francis Galton's forecasting competition" by Kenneth Wallis, Statistical Science, 2014.

[76] In their excellent book *Superforecasting: The Art and Science of Prediction*, Philip E. Tetlock and Dan Gardner Brooday Books, 2016, describe the best practices used by competing teams to make (probabilistic) predictions about anything from elections to the gold price. They recommend that forecasters be accountable for their predictions (and track their accuracy), leave their ego aside, embrace divergence of opinions, and use various sources of information.

[77] Surowiecki initially advised for five factors: diversity of opinion, independence, decentralization, aggregation, and trust. In this book, I boiled this down to three main factors applicable to demand forecasting in supply chains. (Surowiecki, 2005).

Figure 16.5 Wisdom of the crowds' three pillars

Let's discuss these one by one.

OBJECTIVES ALIGNMENT

Let's imagine a group of individuals sharing a common interest in biasing a prediction in the same direction; averaging their predictions won't result in miraculous accuracy. Because they are all biased in the same way, their respective biases won't compensate for each other. Inevitably the final prediction will also be biased. For example, asking a team of colleagues who all have an interest in providing high estimates for future demand won't translate into much added value. The resulting forecast is still likely to be overly optimistic.

For the wisdom of the crowd to work, you need to remove all intentional biases by aligning everyone's objectives. You want everyone in the crowd to give their best shot at estimating the target. Not playing their own hidden games.

In practice, when discussing demand forecasts, make sure that everyone understands what a forecast is (an unconstrained, unbiased prediction of future demand) and what a forecast is not (a supply plan, sales targets, or the budget, see chapter 2). By aligning everyone's KPIs and objectives, you will remove temptations to bias the forecast. For example, a bad practice would be to incentivize salespeople to beat the forecasts—this would incentivize them to under forecast demand to exceed the target and collect bonuses. On the contrary, a good practice would be to keep everyone accountable for their achieved accuracy and bias by tracking FVA (chapter 12).

MINDSET DIVERSITY

At the core of the wisdom of the crowd lies the idea that you want to bring different insights to the table. One of the best ways to do that is to gather different-minded people with diverse backgrounds. By doing so, you can leverage varied points of view because each member will pay attention to different and contradictory information and details. Even if everyone is still likely to be (unconsciously) biased, these biases are likely to be different—compensating for each other.

In practice, when discussing demand forecasts, you could gather colleagues from various departments: sales, marketing, finance, and supply. They will look at the forecasts with unique perspectives and most likely be aware of different information. Moreover, when discussing forecasts, look for colleagues with field knowledge and other colleagues with broader views. For colleagues with quantitative and qualitative mindsets, for optimists and pessimists, and so on.

In short, to enrich your forecast, gather a team with as many different backgrounds and mindsets as possible.

WORKING INDEPENDENTLY

To reap the maximum out of the wisdom of the crowd, you want each team member to work as independently as possible. In practice, each team member needs to work using their own judgment to find pieces of information, assess what is relevant, and how these will impact future demand. In their thought process, team members must not be influenced by anyone or any external statement. Remember, humans are prone to the anchoring bias and, in general, to *groupthink* (figure 16.6). We tend to promote harmony and consensus in groups because we want to fit in and go along with the group. Groups also tend to develop their own identity, to the detriment of independent judgments. Moreover, you do not want to be seen as the pessimist of the group when predicting future incomes. To avoid this, when working on predictions, you should avoid all social, hierarchical, political, or peer pressure. Team members need to feel safe to come up with a different prediction than the rest of the group and won't be blamed, labeled, or excluded for that.[78] Instead, singular predictions, forecasts, or opinions should be welcomed with an open mindset.

As discussed earlier, with the anchoring bias, any random piece of information can potentially alter your judgment. Can you imagine the influence of hearing a remark made by a colleague or reading an email sent by your manager? It is critical to keep each stakeholder as independent as possible from the opinion of other team members and political pressure. By empowering independence, you will get the most out of group forecasting.

In practice, ensure everyone works on their own before sharing their forecasts with the rest of the group.

If your process still suffers from too much peer pressure and influence, you could also use anonymous predictions. For example, you could start a critical S&OP meeting by asking each participant to note down the sales numbers they expect for the next quarter. Then, shuffle the numbers and reveal them to get the discussion started.

---

[78] For a more detailed discussion and examples, see the book *Leadership Is Language: The Hidden Power of What You Say and What You Don't* by L. David Marquet, Portfolio, 2020.

Figure 16.6   Groupthink illustrated by Jono Hey on his website sketchplanations.com

16.3.2   *Assumption-based discussions*

Imagine the following scenario. You read the previous sections on the wisdom of the crowd and decided to organize your next meeting with the following procedure: your three colleagues had to prepare estimates independently in advance and will share them during a joint session (without any prior discussion, so as not to influence anyone). Moreover, you ensured that everyone's objectives were aligned. Your colleagues are forecasting unconstrained demand and doing their best to do it unbiasedly. Everyone could also access and use whatever information they thought fit.

Looking at the numbers, your forecast engine generated a baseline forecast for next month of 1,000 units. As you announce this to your team, they share their estimates: 1,250, 1,300, and 1,150 units (figure 16.7).

How much should your final forecast be?

Figure 16.7   A typical demand forecasting discussion

Take a minute to think about it, and once you set your mind on a final number, continue your reading.

I always ask this question in my training courses, and most attendees—professionals and students alike—reply something in-between 1,150 and 1,250 (figure 16.8).

Figure 16.8   Collaborative forecast by averaging everyone's forecasts

But this is a trick question and scenario: averaging everyone's forecast is not a good idea. As shown in figure 16.9, a simple average would not catch all the valuable insights behind their inputs.

Figure 16.9   Collaborative forecast based on assumptions

Indeed, your colleagues all had different good reasons to increase the baseline forecast. They all got access to specific information, so their respective uplift assumptions should be added rather than averaged. As you add the three uplifts, you would get a total of 1,700—far from the average forecast of around 1,200 units.

VOTE FIRST. DEBATE AFTER.

As we have seen with this example, by leading *assumption-based discussions*, we can go one step beyond the traditional wisdom of the crowds. Instead of simply averaging all predictions, you should discuss everyone's underlying assumptions and how they see their impact on demand.

Indeed, directly discussing final numbers will often be sterile and leave too much room for bias and influence: the loudest person in the room might hijack the conversation or groupthink settle in. Instead, you should discuss the underlying assumptions and leading indicators driving everyone's forecasts: new product launches, marketing budgets, competition, or pricing. (Do not forget to include good and bad news.) Moreover, it is better to discuss *how* your colleagues treated information rather than *what* information they used. For example, instead of asking closed questions such as *"Did you take the upcoming promotion into account?"*, ask open questions such as *"How did you take this promotion into account?"* The ensuing discussion will be much more insightful than a simple *"Yes."*

Additionally, to reduce anchoring bias and groupthink to the minimum, the highest-paid person in the room should ideally be the last one to talk. Who would dare contradict their manager or N+2?

Finally, to foster independence of thought, assumption-based discussions can be combined with preparing numbers in advance and sharing them simultaneously during the meeting.

Summary

Humans can enrich model-generated forecasts using various insights and information that models do not have access to. When doing so, make sure to avoid:

- *Cognitive biases (unintentional biases):* Everyone is subject to cognitive biases. When forecasting demand, pay attention to:
  - *Anchoring bias:* Any external information could easily influence our thought process.
  - *Confirmation bias:* We tend to look for information supporting our current beliefs.
  - *Apophenia:* We see patterns between unrelated events.

- *Misalignment of incentives (intentional biases):* You need to align everyone's objectives. We want to predict *unconstrained unbiased future demand* (not create sales targets or supply plans). To do so, ensure forecasters and demand planners do not have incentives to bias the forecast.
- Biased forecasting process:
  - *One-sided data or assumptions:* Only looking at specific data without a global 365-degree view (such as reviewing current promotions but not previous ones) will result in a skewed forecast.
  - *Selective justifications:* By asking for more justification for positive or negative editions (good or bad news), managers can skew the overall forecasting biased as planners will take fewer risks in editing the forecast in a specific direction.
  - *Imbalance in stakeholders' influence:* Some (group of) colleagues might get too much influence on the final forecast, multiplying the effect of all the other mentioned biases.

You can increase your forecasting quality by including more people in the demand planning process. When gathering a team to generate or edit forecasts pay attention to:

- *Objective alignment:* Remove intentional biases by ensuring no one is interested in skewing forecasts in a specific direction.
- *Mindset diversity:* Bring together people with different mindsets and backgrounds. They are more likely to use different sources of information (bringing different insights to the table), and their biases are more likely to compensate each other.
- *Independence of work:* Let everyone work independently to avoid any social pressure or anchoring bias. Avoid groupthink (*we want to conform to the group*).
- *Assumption-based discussions:* Promote assumption-based discussions where you do not discuss final numbers but underlying assumptions and demand drivers.

In any case, monitoring forecast value added (FVA) is the cornerstone of demand planning excellence because it enforces accountability and ownership (chapter 12). Using it will track the added value of your team and the time they spend working on the forecast.

Now it's your turn!

Chapter after chapter, you learned the best practices that will lead you to demand planning excellence (figure 17.1). These practices will ensure both efficacy (your forecasts are helpful to support your supply chain decisions) and efficiency (your teams work smart, not hard).

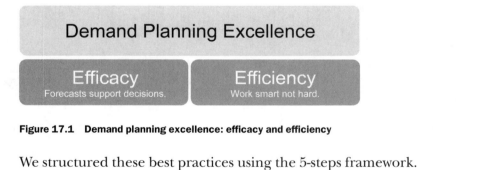

Figure 17.1   Demand planning excellence: efficacy and efficiency

We structured these best practices using the 5-steps framework.

Figure 17.2   5-steps framework for demand planning excellence

Following this framework will structure your improvement journey. Let's recap the five steps.

1 *Objective:* What do you need to forecast?

Start by asking yourself (and your colleagues) what the demand forecast is used for. What decisions are you supporting with this forecast? Once you know these decisions, you can assess the relevant material, geographical, and temporal aggregation levels (chapter 5) and the forecasting horizon (chapter 6).

2 *Data:* What data do you need to support your forecasting model and process?

The second step is to collect relevant data to support your forecast model and process. The most important part is to capture demand rather than sales. We discussed multiple techniques to unconstraint historical sales in chapters 3 and 4. Among other methods, tracking inventory levels and shortages will help you to identify constrained periods. These periods can then be considered as outliers (or *events*) in your forecasting model. In addition, you should also collect data about the demand drivers relevant to your business (promotions, pricing, and marketing, among others; see chapter 14).

3 *Metrics:* How do you evaluate forecasting quality?

Setting up the appropriate metrics to assess your forecasting accuracy is critical. Not using relevant KPIs will leave your team running after irrelevant duties. In Part III, you learned:

- How to track both accuracy and bias.
- To use value-weighted metrics to cope with broad product portfolios.
- To assess your process and model added value, compare yourself against a benchmark (such as a moving average).

These last two elements are often overlooked by practitioners (consultants, planners, and software vendors alike). Do not make this mistake.

4 *Baseline model:* How do you create an accurate, automated forecast baseline?

To increase your forecasting accuracy and reduce your team workload, you have to set up a forecasting model that will leverage the data you collected in step 2. This model will do the heavy lifting for you by automatically generating most (if not all) forecasts. As you include more demand drivers in your forecasting engine, your team will have to spend less time reviewing forecasts for exceptions, and you will enjoy a more accurate forecast baseline. Two birds, one stone.

If your dataset is limited (a few hundred SKUs, not much historical data, and no demand drivers), you should first try the usual time series models (chapter 14). On the other hand, if you could collect demand drivers or enjoy a larger dataset, machine learning might be able to capture more complex relationships (chapter 15).

5 *Review process:* How do you review the baseline forecast, and who should do it?

Tracking forecast value added (FVA) is the cornerstone of demand-planning excellence. It promotes accountability and ownership. And helps managers monitor the overall process, ensuring that it adds value and runs efficiently.

To reduce the workload of your team and increase the quality of your forecasts, you need to ensure that:

- Various team members review the baseline forecast with different points of view using diverse sources of information (chapter 16).
- Reduce intentional biases to the minimum by aligning everyone's objectives. Start by explaining what a demand forecast is and is not (chapter 2).
- Avoid cognitive biases and leverage the wisdom of the crowd by aligning everyone's objectives, cultivating mindset diversity, and fostering independence of work and judgment.
- When discussing forecasts, discuss underlying assumptions and resulting impacts rather than focusing on end numbers.
- People working on the forecast should focus on where they are the most likely to add value. An effective ABC XYZ classification will help you to pinpoint the products that should be reviewed first. As explained in chapter 13, to segment your products, avoid tracking historical volumes or demand variation. Instead, use historical forecast errors and expected revenues (or costs).

Closing words

Dear reader, you have now reached the end of *Demand Forecasting Best Practices.* I hope you enjoyed this journey and found it useful for your professional endeavors.

I would love to hear how you applied these ideas and techniques. You can reach me at nicolas.vandeput@supchains.com or on LinkedIn.

references

Bojer, C. S., & Meldgaard, J. P. (2021). "Kaggle forecasting competitions: An overlooked learning opportunity". *International Journal of Forecasting*, 37.

Bowman, R. J. (2013). "There Is No Magic Number for Demand Forecasting". *SupplyChainBrain*. Retrieved December 17, 2020, from https://www.supplychainbrain.com/blogs/1-think-tank/post/15929-there-is-no-magic-number-for-demand-forecasting

Chen, T., & Guestrin, C. (2016). "XGBoost: A Scalable Tree Boosting System". In *Proceedings of the 22nd ACM SIGKDD International Conference on Knowledge Discovery and Data Mining* (pp. 785-794). ACM.

Clarke, S. (2019). "One-number forecasting". *Argon&Co*. Retrieved December 17, 2020, from https://www.argonandco.com/us/news-insights/articles/one-number-forecasting-sandy-springs-atlanta-ga/

Conrad, K. (1958). *Die beginnende Schizophrenie* [Journal]. Thieme Verlag.

Desmet, B. (2018). *Supply Chain Strategy and Financial Metrics: The Supply Chain Triangle Of Service Cost And Cash*. Kogan Page.

Fildes, R., & Goodwin, P. (2007). *"Good and Bad Judgment in Forecasting: Lessons from Four Companies"*. *Foresight*.

Freund, Y., & Schapire, R. E. (1997). "A Decision-Theoretic Generalization of On-Line Learning and an Application to Boosting". *Journal of Computer and System Sciences*, 55.

Gardner, E. S., & Mckenzie, E. (1985). "Forecasting Trends in Time Series". *Management Science*, 31.

Gilliland, M. (2002). "Is forecasting a waste of time?" *Supply Chain Management Review*.

Gilliland, M. (2010). *The Business Forecasting Deal: Exposing Myths, Eliminating Bad Practices, Providing Practical Solutions*. John Wiley & Sons.

Holt, C. C. (2004). "Forecasting seasonals and trends by exponentially weighted moving averages". *International Journal of Forecasting*, 20.

Hyndman, R. J. (2018). "A brief history of time series forecasting competitions". *Hyndsight*. Retrieved October 22, 2022, from https://robjhyndman.com/hyndsight/forecasting-competitions/.

Hyndman, R. J., & Athanasopoulos, G. (2021). *Forecasting: Principles and Practice* [Book].

Ke, G., Meng, Q., Finley, T., Wang, T., Chen, W., Ma, W., & Ye, Q. (2017). "LightGBM: A Highly Efficient Gradient Boosting Decision Tree". In *Advances in Neural Information Processing Systems* (pp. 3146-3154).

Kendall, G. (2019, September 11). "The First Moon Landing Was Achieved with Less Computing Power Than a Cell Phone or a Calculator". *Pacific Standard. Retrieved October 22, 2022, from* https://psmag.com/social-justice/ground-control-to-major-tim-cook.

Kolassa, S. (2008). "Can We Obtain Valid Benchmarks from Published Surveys of Forecast Accuracy". *Foresight.*

Le Cunff, A. (2019). "Confirmation bias: believing what you see, seeing what you believe". *Ness Labs.* Retrieved October 22, 2022, from https://nesslabs.com/confirmation-bias.

LeCun, Y., Boser, B., Denker, J. S., Henderson, D., Howard, R. E., Hubbard, W., & Jackel, L. D. (1989). "Backpropagation applied to handwritten zip code recognition". *Neural computation,* 1(4), 541-551.

Makridakis, S., Spiliotis, E., & Assimakopoulos, V. (2022). "The M5 Accuracy competition: Results, findings and conclusions". *International Journal of Forecasting, 38(1), 209-223.*

Marquet, D. L. (2020). *Leadership Is Language: The Hidden Power of What You Say and What You Don't* [Journal]. Portfolio.

McRaney David. "Anchoring Effect" [Online] *You Are Not So Smart. - July 27, 2010. - October 22, 2022. -* https://youarenotsosmart.com/2010/07/27/anchoring-effect/.

Mello, John. (2009). "The Impact of Sales Forecast Game Playing on Supply Chains". *Foresight,* Spring, 13.

Morgan, J. A., & Sonquist, J. N. (1963). "Problems in the Analysis of Survey Data, and a Proposal". *Journal of the American Statistical Association, 58(302), 415-434.*

Oliva, R. and Watson, N. (2009) "Managing Functional Biases in Organizational Forecasts: A Case Study of Consensus Forecasting in Supply Chain Planning", *Production and Operations Management,* 2.

Pedregosa, F., Varoquaux, G., Gramfort, A., Michel, V., Thirion, B., Grisel, O., ... & Vanderplas, J. (2011). "Scikit-learn: Machine Learning in Python". *Journal of Machine Learning Research, 12, 2825-2830.*

Rosenblatt, F. (1957) "The perceptron, a perceiving and recognizing automaton Project Para". Cornell Aeronautical Laboratory, Journal.

Rumelhart, D. E., Hinton, G. E., & Williams, R. J. (1986). "Learning representations by back-propagating errors". *Nature, 323(6088), 533-536.*

Surowiecki, J. (2005) *The Wisdom of Crowds,* Anchor.

Tetlock, P. E. and Gardner, D. (2016) *Superforecasting: The Art and Science of Prediction,* Broadway Books.

Vandeput, N. (2020). *Inventory Optimization: Models and Simulations.* De Gruyter.

Vandeput, N. (2021). *Data Science for Supply Chain Forecasting.* De Gruyter.

Wallis, K. F. (2014) "Revisiting Francis Galton's forecasting competition", JSTOR.

Wason, P. C. (1960) "On the failure to eliminate hypotheses in a conceptual task", SAGE Publications.

Werbos, P. (1974) "Beyond regression: New tools for prediction and analysis in the behavioral sciences", PhD dissertation, Harvard University.

Winters, P. R. (1960). "Forecasting Sales by Exponentially Weighted Moving Averages". Management Science, 6(3), 324-342.

index

Demand forecast, supply plans, and sales

Demand Forecasting Best Practices

Nicolas Vandeput

An expert demand forecaster can help an organization avoid overproduction, reduce waste, and optimize inventory levels for a real competitive advantage. This book teaches you how to become that virtuoso demand forecaster.

Demand Forecasting Best Practices reveals forecasting tools, metrics, models, and stakeholder management techniques for managing your demand planning process efficiently and effectively. Everything you learn has been proven and tested in a live business environment. Discover author Nicolas Vandeput's original five step framework for demand planning excellence and learn how to tailor it to your own company's needs. Illustrations and real-world examples make each concept easy to understand and easy to follow. You'll soon be delivering accurate predictions that are driving major business value.

What's Inside

- Enhance forecasting quality while reducing team workload
- Utilize intelligent KPIs to track accuracy and bias
- Identify process areas for improvement
- Assist stakeholders in sales, marketing, and finance
- Optimize statistical and machine learning models

For demand planners, sales and operations managers, supply chain leaders, and data scientists.

Nicolas Vandeput is a supply chain data scientist, the founder of consultancy company SupChains in 2016, and a teacher at CentraleSupélec, France.

For print book owners, all ebook formats are free:
https://www.manning.com/freebook

> **"**Illustrates how the Forecast Value Added framework drives efficiency and effectiveness in the forecasting process.**"**
> —Michael Gilliland
> Editor-in-Chief, Foresight: Journal of Applied Forecasting

> **"**A must-read for any SCM professional, data scientist and business owner.**"**
> —Edouard Thieuleux
> Founder of AbcSupplyChain

> **"**From basic principles to advanced forecasting techniques. An exceptional resource.**"**
> —Daniel Stanton
> Mr. Supply Chain®

> **"**Provides practical advice for improving your demand planning process.**"**
> —Spyros Makridakis,
> The Makridakis Open Forecasting Center, Institute For the Future (IFF), University of Nicosia

Free eBook
See first page

ISBN-13: 978-1-63343-809-5

90000

9 781633 438095

MANNING